T0062607

EXECUTIVE FUNCTIONING ACTIVITIES

EXECUTIVE FUNCTIONING ACTIVITIES

Exercises and Strategies to Engage Your Child and Help Them Organize Their Thoughts

MELISSA ROSE, LPC-MHSP, NCC

ROCKRIDGE PRESS

No book, including this one, can ever replace the diagnostic expertise and medical advice of a physician in providing information about your health. The information contained herein is not intended to replace medical advice. You should consult with your doctor before using the information in this or any health-related book.

Copyright © 2022 by Rockridge Press

All rights reserved. No part of this publication may be reproduced, stored in a retrieval system, or transmitted in any form or by any means, electronic, mechanical, photocopying, recording, scanning, or otherwise without the prior written permission of the Publisher. Requests to the Publisher for permission should be addressed to the Permissions Department, Rockridge Press, 1955 Broadway, Suite 400, Oakland, CA 94612.

First Rockridge Press trade paperback edition 2022

Rockridge Press and the Rockridge Press logo are trademarks or registered trademarks of Callisto Media Inc. and/or its affiliates in the United States and other countries and may not be used without written permission.

For general information on our other products and services, please contact our Customer Care Department within the United States at (866) 744-2665, or outside the United States at (510) 253-0500.

Paperback ISBN: 978-1-63878-747-1 | eBook ISBN: 978-1-68539-118-8

Manufactured in the United States of America

Interior and Cover Designer: Linda Snorina
Art Producer: Sue Bischofberger
Editor: Mo Mozuch
Production Editor: Jaime Chan
Production Manager: Lanore Coloprisco

Illustrations used under license from shutterstock.com
Author photo courtesy of Tassi Williams Photography

10 9 8 7 6 5 4 3 2 1 0

This book is dedicated to
the millions of children around
the world who silently struggle
with an executive function disorder.

CONTENTS

INTRODUCTION viii

HOW TO USE THIS BOOK ix

PART I: Understanding Executive Functioning in Kids 1

CHAPTER 1: What Parents Need to Know about Executive Functioning 3

CHAPTER 2: How to Use Positive Techniques to Build Executive Functioning 19

PART II: Executive Functioning Games and Activities 29

CHAPTER 3: Master Your Impulses 31

CHAPTER 4: Make Your Memory Work for You 49

CHAPTER 5: Manage Your Emotions 67

CHAPTER 6: Improve Your Attention Span 87

CHAPTER 7: Learn How to Start Tasks 105

CHAPTER 8: Practice Planning and Prioritizing 125

CHAPTER 9: Get Organized 143

CHAPTER 10: Stay Flexible 161

CLOSING THOUGHTS 179

RESOURCES 180

REFERENCES 181

INDEX 183

INTRODUCTION

When I was a child, I can remember thinking, "It's not supposed to be this hard." My peers balanced life with so much ease, whereas I was constantly daydreaming, misplacing things, and forgetting important details. I couldn't seem to retain information and would frequently respond with "I don't remember." With low expectations for my academic performance, and a stifled compassion for my ever-growing brain, I sincerely believed that I was unintelligent. I remember wishing that I could have a new brain that actually worked.

I grew up in a time when mental health was stigmatized, and there were many misconceptions about learning disabilities. Although studies on disorders such as ADHD were producing promising data in the 1990s, there was a significant flaw in the research that greatly impacted young girls like me. For various reasons, girls with ADHD were often overlooked. Early research on gender differences in ADHD attributed the common misdiagnosis to variations in how the disorder manifests among boys and girls. Essentially, girls diagnosed with ADHD show fewer hyperactive/impulsive symptoms and more inattentive symptoms. This continues to cause difficulties in the detection and diagnosis of girls with ADHD.

Studying psychology in undergrad led me to realize that I didn't need a new brain—I needed modified study habits and a change in perspective. With a renewed sense of self and love for learning, I graduated with a master's in mental health counseling in 2015 and soon became a board-certified, licensed professional counselor. I spent several years treating children and families in a community mental health setting and gradually transitioned to private practice. Today, I have dedicated nearly a decade to my work with children.

My hope for this workbook is that it provides you with a sense of understanding and empowerment that you may be lacking right now. The activities in this book have been designed with many children in mind and cover a wide range of issues. From preschoolers to school-age children, those with a formal diagnosis and those without, this workbook is a great tool for any child ages four to twelve who struggles with executive skills. Let's get started!

HOW TO USE THIS BOOK

This workbook is divided into two parts for easier navigation. Part 1 introduces parents to the concept of executive functioning skills and discusses in detail the challenges that children often face when these skills are absent. Part 2 focuses on a variety of games and activities that parents can do with their child to improve these skills.

The activities are organized by level of difficulty in each chapter, with the more basic activities and games at the beginning of the chapter and progressing to the intermediate level and most advanced. Exercises at the beginning of each chapter may be more appropriate for younger kids than exercises at the end, but parents should move through the book at their child's pace. You'll also see some exercises flagged as an "On The Page Activity"; these are fill-in-the-blank pages you can work on together.

Some things may appear fun and easy, but remember these cognitive exercises can be mentally draining for your child. As you work through this book, keep a close eye on your child's behavior and attitude toward the new skills. If they seem to be getting easily frustrated, upset, or overwhelmed by an activity, it may be time to take a break or save it for another day.

Make these exercises a positive experience! Carve out time in your day to give your child undivided attention. You could offer a special snack during this time or use a form of positive reinforcement that has worked well in the past. Much like learning any new skill, these activities may take time and repetition for your child to grasp them. Pair this book with plenty of patience and praise, and you will set the stage for your child's success!

PART I

UNDERSTANDING EXECUTIVE FUNCTIONING IN KIDS

The brain and the body share an intimate connection. In order to better understand your child's behaviors, we must first closely examine the biological processes that propel them. The brain is a uniquely complex organ, so it's important to understand that childhood brain development is fluid and will occur at various rates. And let's be honest, you didn't come here to study neuroscience, so I will keep the information as simple as possible. Read over this section to gain a clearer understanding of your child's development and how it relates to their behavior, and refer back to it anytime you find yourself asking, "Why on earth did they do that?"

CHAPTER 1

What Parents Need to Know about Executive Functioning

You're probably anxious to dive right in to the lessons, but resist the temptation to jump ahead. These next few pages will offer meaningful information that will help you understand the chapters to come. We'll look at a real-life scenario of a child who came to me with executive functioning difficulties, then explore how these skills are developed, why they sometimes don't, and what you can look forward to as you help your child improve.

BOTTLING UP FEELINGS

Ashley initially came to me for treatment following a year of issues at school. She had just completed first grade, and her parents were concerned about her classroom behavior and work habits. Ashley's teacher would often report that she would daydream in class, doodle on her work, and forget directions despite having been told multiple times. Ashley would often fall behind in her classwork and sometimes needed to finish assignments during recess. Her parents noticed she would often come home exhausted and moody, which commonly resulted in tension within the family. Over time, Ashley became discouraged and seemed to lack healthy self-esteem.

Although everyone wanted to help Ashley, they just weren't sure how to do it. During my initial therapy intake, Ashley presented as a bright and bubbly seven-year-old who was eager to please. After receiving the results of the assessments from Ashley's teacher and parents, Ashley was diagnosed with attention deficit hyperactivity disorder (ADHD), with the inattentive subtype. Through a combination of play therapy and cognitive behavioral therapy (CBT), Ashley learned effective strategies for controlling her thoughts and behaviors, and regulating her emotions. Since beginning treatment, she has received praise reports from her teacher, improved her grades, and appears more confident in herself.

What Are Executive Skills?

Think for a moment about the responsibilities that you have on a day-to-day basis. From maintaining a routine to juggling many jobs at once to managing your emotions, these important components keep your life running smoothly. What you likely attribute to being a responsible adult are, in fact, a set of neurological processes called "executive functioning." These skills contribute to a more structured, meaningful, and productive thought process. A good way to think about it is like a crossing guard managing a busy intersection. It is their job to ensure that traffic runs smoothly by directing who can proceed and when. Similarly, the brain relies on these skills to organize, prioritize, and rationalize thinking.

This all happens in an area of the brain known as the "prefrontal cortex." Located just behind your forehead, it is unique in that it develops at a much slower rate than its counterparts. As this part of the brain grows, so do the skills it controls. For a neurotypical child, the executive skills usually emerge in a similar order. Beginning with impulse control, then working memory, emotional control, sustained attention and goal-oriented persistence, task initiation, planning and prioritization, organization, and, finally, flexibility. You will notice that the activities in part 2 of this book will maintain this same order. Each executive skill plays an important role in daily operations. Let's take a closer look at the purpose each of them serves.

Impulse Control

Impulse control is the ability to pause and think before responding to a situation. Anytime that you have paused to consider the options, stopped before blurting out something hurtful, or chosen a healthy snack over junk food is a time that you have controlled your impulse. This is also the skill necessary for children to make safe decisions, such as stopping before following a ball into a busy road.

Working Memory

Working memory is the ability to retain and recall information while completing a task. This skill is important for a variety of everyday tasks such as cooking, cleaning, and driving a vehicle. For children, working memory allows them to accomplish things like homework and learning a new sport.

Emotional Control

Emotional control is the ability to acknowledge your thoughts and feelings and maintain a healthy level of comfortability and control. Having the ability to consistently regulate your own emotions is a superpower in the sense that you have complete control over how you respond to your environment. Children with ADHD, such as Ashley, have a tendency to use every ounce of available energy to control their emotions during school. Then when the child enters a safe and supportive environment such as home, their emotions spew out like a shaken can of soda. Sometimes it can appear as the child coming home with a bad attitude, whereas other times it may be that they are bouncing off the walls. Children with advanced self-regulation skills can set out to conquer any goal without the limitations of unpredictable emotions.

Sustained Attention and Goal-Oriented Persistence

Sustained attention and goal-oriented persistence is how adults maintain focus on one important matter at a time. Without second thought, this skill enables us to dismiss irrelevant ideas similar to the way that we dismiss notifications on our cell phone. We may take a brief look, but we quickly return to the task at hand. This is one of the important skills that begin to emerge in elementary-age children. Students who are good listeners in the classroom and can complete their assignments with limited assistance are likely to feel more confident and content during their time at school.

Task Initiation

Similarly, the skill of task initiation is significant for academic success. Children who lack the ability or motivation to start assignments on their own will often fall behind. Many children with ADHD are excellent self-starters when it comes to preferred activities; however, they may struggle to know where to begin on tasks that seem difficult. Task initiation is having the ability to see something that needs to be done and doing it.

Planning and Prioritization

Planning and prioritizing is another important skill that adults use almost constantly. Young children, on the other hand, will need extra assistance in this area for many years. This is because children don't typically gain this capability until around adolescence and will get better at it as they grow into young adults.

Organization

Being organized is typically not a young child's strong suit, either. During early childhood, the limited set of executive skills makes organization difficult. Organization is one of the final executive functions to develop and offers us the ability to create and maintain order. Even adults can experience difficulties with this skill, so it's important to set realistic expectations based on the child's developmental ability.

Flexibility

Finally, cognitive flexibility is the way that we can "switch gears" and keep going with our day. This skill is often the final to develop as it requires more abstract thinking. So, it equips us with the ability to change perspectives, consider alternatives, and reevaluate our thoughts. Children who are flexible thinkers are usually go-with-the-flow problem-solvers who are open to new ideas.

Supplemental Skills

The following terms are used throughout the book to describe additional skills that are essential to your child's development. You can think of executive functioning as the trunk of the tree with many important branches of skills that extend out. As your child strengthens their executive skills, these competencies will follow. From conversations to playing a board game, these abilities will help set your child up for success.

Following Directions

The ability for a child to follow the first request from a parent carries a significance beyond just being compliant. It is a foundational skill that is built on safety and trust and grows into an understanding of responsibility and respect for others.

Turn-Taking

The ability to pause and wait during social interactions is an important skill that children must learn from an early age. As they gain the ability to take turns in their play, they will simultaneously sharpen their executive skills, such as impulse control and emotional regulation.

Attention to Detail

For matters of safety and success, a child needs the ability to home in on important details and use that information effectively. This is especially true once the child begins school. Practicing executive skills such as impulse control and working memory can help children focus on the details and avoid making "careless mistakes."

Imagination

A common strength of children who struggle with executive functioning is creativity, or having the ability to bring unique ideas to life. The art of imagination has no bounds and allows a child who is often limited by their abilities to express themselves in a meaningful way.

Problem-Solving

Finding a solution to a problem can be a complex task, especially for children. The ability to problem-solve requires the executive skills of working memory, planning and prioritization, and mental flexibility. Children typically sharpen this skill over time as they are presented with obstacles in daily life.

Frustration Tolerance

Frustration tolerance is the ability or inability to stay emotionally balanced when success is out of reach. When faced with a challenge, stress can quickly grow into anger when uncontrolled. Children need emotional regulation skills in order to maintain a healthy frustration tolerance.

How Do Executive Skills Develop in Children?

When children are born, the expectation is that the parent should teach them how to successfully operate within the world around them. What is often misunderstood is how much we can expect from children and when. You can find perfect examples of this on any social media platform, where there are endless amounts of posts, groups, and pages talking about how to parent a child effectively. Unfortunately, kids don't come equipped with a how-to guide, and raising a child is hard. It's difficult to know where to look and who to believe.

Think of the expectations that you require of the child(ren) in your life—for example, picking up their toys, asking for help, and using crayons properly (not on walls). These are all tasks that require executive skills. It's hard to know what a child is capable of since there is no external light that turns on telling us when a child's executive functions are working properly. What we do know is that a child's development depends on both internal (biological) and external (environmental and experiential) factors.

Biological Factors

According to researchers, executive functions are among the most inheritable psychological traits. This means that parents with strong organization skills will likely have children who are naturally more organized. Parents with weaknesses in areas such as emotion regulation or task initiation will likely pass on those difficulties to their children. An additional biological factor that may play a role is the child's sex. Research has attributed this to female brains often maturing more quickly and beginning to process information much sooner than boys.

Environmental Factors

Research has shown that factors such as a child's living arrangements, family income, educational opportunities, and access to health care can all play a large role in the proper functioning and growth of a child's brain and body. Consider the foundation that executive function skills are built on, such as healthy nutrition, love, safety, and adequate sleep. A child who lacks basic needs being met will be most focused on satisfying those needs first. All other skills and processes must take a back seat. Unfortunately, when this cycle repeats itself due to a toxic environment, the result can be an underdeveloped brain and nervous system.

ASSESSMENT OF EXECUTIVE SKILLS IN CHILDREN AGES FOUR TO EIGHT

Take a look at these eight key executive functions and issues that commonly impact children at this age. Circle those that are true for your child. Please note: This assessment is meant to be a guide for effectively using the activities in this book and does not take the place of an official diagnosis.

IMPULSE CONTROL

Hyperactive	Difficulty sitting still	Touches everything in the store

EMOTION REGULATION

Easily frustrated	Frequent tantrums	Irritability

TASK INITIATION

Needs multiple reminders	Lacks motivation	Doesn't play well independently

ORGANIZATION

Room is excessively messy	Puts toys in the wrong place	Poor time management

WORKING MEMORY

Difficulty transitioning from one thing to another	Struggles with problem-solving	Difficulty following multistep directions

SUSTAINED ATTENTION/GOAL-ORIENTED PERSISTENCE

Easily distracted	Moves quickly from one activity to the next	Daydreams or doesn't seem to listen

PLANNING AND PRIORITIZING

Difficulty with stacking or building	Completes homework, crafts, etc. out of order	Overlooks important details

FLEXIBILITY

Sensitive to change	Rigid (black-and-white) thinking	Resistant to new ideas or strategies

Interpreting the results: Total the number of issues circled under each key area. Those with one or more are likely the most impactful for your child. The higher the impact, the more significant the challenges on your child's daily functioning. Consider spending more time practicing the skills under the coordinating chapters. *For example: A child with one or more issues under Impulse Control would benefit from the activities in chapter 3, Master Your Impulses.*

1 = Mild Impact, **2** = Moderate Impact, **3** = Severe Impact

Keep in mind that every child develops at their own pace, and many of these issues can be a part of normal development.

ASSESSMENT OF EXECUTIVE SKILLS IN CHILDREN AGES EIGHT TO TWELVE

Take a look at these eight key executive functions and issues that commonly impact children at this age. Circle those that are true for your child. Please note: This assessment is meant to be a guide for effectively using the activities in this book and does not take the place of an official diagnosis.

IMPULSE CONTROL

Hyperactive	Difficulty sitting still	Interrupts conversations

EMOTION REGULATION

Easily frustrated/irritable	Sensitive to criticism	Anxious/worries about things

TASK INITIATION

Needs multiple reminders	Lacks motivation	Procrastinates

ORGANIZATION

Room is excessively messy	Often struggles to find belongings	Poor time management

WORKING MEMORY

Difficulty transitioning from one thing to another	Struggles with problem-solving	Difficulty following multistep directions

SUSTAINED ATTENTION/GOAL-ORIENTED PERSISTENCE

Easily distracted	Gives up easily	Daydreams or doesn't seem to listen

PLANNING AND PRIORITIZING

Often has missing homework assignments	Completes homework, crafts, etc. out of order	Overlooks important details

FLEXIBILITY

Sensitive to change	Easily overwhelmed by a problem	Resistant to new ideas or strategies

Interpreting the results: Total the number of issues circled under each key area. Those with one or more are likely the most impactful for your child. The higher the impact, the more significant the challenges on your child's daily functioning. Consider spending more time practicing the skills under the coordinating chapters. *For example: A child with one or more issues under Emotion Regulation would benefit from the activities in chapter 5, Manage Your Emotions.*

1 = Mild Impact, **2** = Moderate Impact, **3** = Severe Impact

Keep in mind that every child develops at their own pace, and many of these issues can be a part of normal development.

Experiential Factors

Positive interactions can offer children the confidence and understanding to effectively use executive skills. Negative experiences that are perceived as uncomfortable or stressful, however, can have lasting effects on a child's executive functioning. When fear is introduced into any scenario, the natural tendency is for the body to shut down nonessential processes and activate our survival skills. If this occurs too often or to a child who is already emotionally hypersensitive, it can significantly hinder the development of executive skills.

Does Your Child Need to Strengthen Their Executive Skills?

Child development is a fluid process that is unique for each individual and dependent on a multitude of factors. As we have already discussed, some children are predisposed to executive functioning issues, whereas others may have negative experiences that cause problems down the road. Many parents begin having concerns early on, such as when their toddler is displaying frequent tantrums or their preschooler can't sit still during circle time. Sometimes learning delays or cognitive deficits may go unnoticed until the child enters school. One of the first big tests of a child's cognitive and emotional abilities is how they respond to the classroom environment.

For many families, having a child enter school is one of the most exciting yet stressful times in their life. There's a sense of vulnerability that comes with entrusting another adult with your child, especially if their behavior can be somewhat problematic at times. The parent-teacher bond is meant to be a dynamic partnership that can work in everyone's favor. It's important to keep in mind that your child's teacher is one of their biggest fans and a key evaluator of their executive skills. Coordinate with their teacher as much as possible. I created the following assessments to help you narrow down which executive functioning challenges your child may be facing. The results may help guide your journey as you work through this book with your child. Keep in mind that it's always best to seek help from a mental health professional if you feel a formal assessment/diagnosis would be beneficial.

HOW TO BE A GOOD ROLE MODEL FOR PRACTICING EXECUTIVE FUNCTIONING

Children will often pick up on their parents' habits for completing day-to-day tasks. For this reason, it's essential that parents model healthy practices for getting things done.

Keep a family calendar posted somewhere in the home and empower the kids to help keep it updated.

Try using brightly colored markers or stickers to capture their interest.

- Allow your child to observe you making grocery lists or to-do lists.
- Be more open to showing emotion. It's important that your child sees ALL feelings as a normal part of life, not just the comfortable ones.
- Speaking of feelings, talk about them often. Reflect on how a friend made you feel or how certain things get under your skin.
- Allow your child to observe you using healthy coping strategies (deep breathing, taking a break, talking through an issue, etc.).
- Take the scenic route home just for fun.
- Invite the entire family in on planning a future event, such as a vacation, a big move, etc.
- Talk about the executive skills that you find most difficult. Name the shortcuts or strategies that you found to be the most effective. It's likely that your child will find validation and a deeper understanding of themselves through your transparency.

What's a Diagnosis Got to Do with It?

Childhood mental health requires reaching developmental and emotional milestones while learning healthy social skills. Children with sound mental health regularly use healthy coping strategies and can effectively problem-solve issues. For many kids with childhood mental health disorders such as attention deficit hyperactivity disorder (ADHD), autism spectrum disorder, generalized anxiety disorder, or any other learning disability, the already immature prefrontal cortex is underfunctioning and causing mild to severe delays in development. In fact, research has shown that children with ADHD have a prefrontal cortex that is about five years behind schedule.

Although mental health disorders can cause executive functioning issues, children of all ages and levels of functioning can struggle. Typically, children with a formal diagnosis will require professional help, such as psychotherapy or medication management; however, mental health services are not always the most accessible for everyone. The beauty of this book is that it provides many CBT-based concepts and skills that clinicians use in the therapeutic setting. Although it does not take the place of professional treatment, it can offer similar support and insight.

How Working on Executive Functioning Skills Will Help Your Child and You

A strong set of executive skills will enable a child to be their best self. Suddenly, the child who dreaded going to school before becomes a child who looks forward to their time in class. Parents may notice that their child is more responsible, even-tempered, and proactive at home. With improved executive skills, children can feel more confident in their ability to meet expectations and goals, resulting in increased positive experiences and a healthier self-esteem.

By giving your child the gift of your time, you are showing them that they are a priority. By walking them through each of these skills and participating with them in the provided activities, you are showing them the importance of practice makes progress. Each day that you open this book and return to your child's side, you are proving to them just how committed you are to their success.

Key Takeaways

Executive function skills are an essential part of everyday life. From the moment we wake up to the moment before bed and all the many hours in between, we are working hard using executive skills to reach our own unique goals. For children, executive skills are an essential piece of the developmental puzzle that leads to successful functioning in the many settings of childhood.

- The area of the brain in charge of controlling the executive function is called the prefrontal cortex. It is unique in that it develops at a much slower rate than its counterparts. As this part of the brain grows, so do the skills it controls.
- The eight key executive functions that typically develop in a similar order are: impulse control, working memory, emotion regulation, sustained attention and goal-oriented persistence, task initiation, planning and prioritizing, organization, and flexibility.
- Although children aren't born with these skills, they are born with the capacity to develop them. The development of these skills is dependent upon both internal (biological) and external (environmental and experiential) factors.
- These skills slowly begin to form during the early stages of development and continue to strengthen through the mid to late twenties.
- The parent-teacher bond is a dynamic partnership that can work in everyone's favor. It's important to keep in mind that your child's teacher is one of your child's biggest fans and one of the best evaluators of their executive skills. Use that resource whenever necessary.

CHAPTER 2

How to Use Positive Techniques to Build Executive Functioning

Positive psychology tells us that the way we frame our thoughts and words are highly impactful on ourselves and those around us. This is especially true when it comes to parenting. In this chapter, I will discuss the use of positive techniques, such as praise and reward systems, and why they are effective for improving your child's executive functioning and overall behavior. I will discuss the dos and don'ts of communicating with your child and offer specific strategies to keep your child encouraged and motivated. These constructive approaches are essential tools in the effective parenting tool kit and can be used for this book and beyond.

OVERCOMING ADVERSITY THROUGH POSITIVITY

Camila was a ten-year-old client who just moved to the United States from Colombia with her two teenage sisters and her grandmother. Her grandmother had signed Camila up for therapy following the teacher's recommendation to help Camila cope with the transition. Her grandmother explained that Camila was constantly starting fights with her sisters, staying in her room, and refusing to speak at school. After further investigation, Camila was feeling extremely lonely, jealous of her teenage sisters, and missing the close relationship she used to have with her grandmother. Since moving to the United States, Camila's grandmother had been working long hours, leaving her sisters in charge in the evenings. With Camila's consent, her grandmother also came to therapy to learn more about this issue and receive positive techniques for improving her relationship with Camila. Soon after, her grandmother was able to make adjustments to her schedule to ensure quality time with her family, and Camila was able to better cope with the changes.

Why It's Important to Take a Positive Approach

When you approach someone with compassion and kindness, they are more likely to want to help. It goes back to the study of positive psychology, which says that all people want to lead meaningful and fulfilling lives. By nature, human beings want to feel a sense of success and purpose. Specifically, your child wants to meet your expectations, and they want to make you proud. This is an important notion to remember when you're working with your child. Truly, they are always doing their best with the tools that they have. As adults, sometimes we forget this, which can create an unpleasant interaction. It's hard to see things from their perspective because our brains are so different. Not to mention life is extremely busy and requires parents to think and move quickly. So, when it comes time to slow down and offer patience to your child, it can be difficult and frustrating. Here are some effective solutions to these common parenting challenges.

Don't Blame Your Child for Their Deficits

Having a child with a disability of any kind is an added challenge for parents. Not only does it require extra patience and energy as well as the added stress of coordinating with medical and education services, it requires a change in communication. What words should you use to convey the disability to your child? How do you offer compassion while instilling responsibility? These are valid questions that many parents wrestle with. The best approach is sticking to the facts. Use the proper terminology or diagnosis when discussing your child's challenges. The key is to remove any belief that their delays reflect their overall self. Imperfections are like a freckle or a mole. They may be a part of us, but they don't define us.

Make Sense of Inconsistent Performance

Many learning, social, and emotional challenges of childhood can be attributed to underdeveloped executive function skills. From poor grades to friendship drama to their disorganized room, executive skills are a necessary part of life. When a child has a diagnosis that impacts the development of their executive functioning, the impact can be seen in almost every setting. Keeping this in mind can make a positive difference in the relationship with your child. Maintaining a more positive and compassionate mindset will encourage your child to stay positive and offer themselves compassion, too.

Manage Parental Frustration

Are you reaching the end of your day and realizing that you have no emotional energy left? Or maybe you notice that your patience is usually limited and your frustration tolerance is low. These are indications that your mental health needs some TLC. Increasing your self-care regimen could also help. Finding a healthy regimen to take care of your own emotional well-being is vital to being an effective parent, so you may want to consider seeking out a therapist or life coach. And in the moment, remember to take a breath. Walk away if you need to. You've got this.

Choose Positive Motivation over Negative Consequences

Studies have shown that positive reinforcement is the best approach for children with executive function difficulties. When offering praise, use their name or the specific behavior to add genuine meaning ("I am so proud of you, Natalie"). Keep in mind that setting your child up for success means keeping expectations reasonable and offering reminders often, and, yes, you still need to enforce some boundaries to establish consequences. Be mindful of your child's needs and when all else fails, reset and try again.

Understanding Motivation

Children require inspiration to get things accomplished. These motivating factors must either come from an external (extrinsic) or internal (intrinsic) source. I'll define these in a bit more detail a little later. For now, I want to address the importance of keeping your child motivated. To understand a child's perspective, we can simply examine our own experiences. Think of a time when you were trying something new, such as establishing an exercise regimen or growing your own garden. Think about how it felt emotionally and what you needed to remain committed to your goal. Now think about the interests of a child. Consider how significant playtime and friendships are to them. Their world revolves around fun, so anything outside of that remains less important. Fun is the key ingredient to keeping your child engaged and interested.

As you proceed through this workbook, you may feel inclined to set new regimens, expectations, and procedures into place. In fact, I encourage you to consider ways that you can incorporate the information and strategies that you learn in this book into your child's daily life. Remember that change can be hard, especially when you're asking your child to stretch their capabilities. Keeping your child motivated and building their confidence will be integral to helping them improve. Monitor their attitude toward the workbook and take frequent breaks for freestyle family fun throughout the week. It's always a good idea to consider your child's individual interests and use them to their benefit. Take a moment to complete the short assessment to further explore what motivates your child.

MOTIVATION ASSESSMENT

Examine the common intrinsic and extrinsic motivators for young children listed here. Number the items 1 to 20 (1 = Least, 20 = Most) based on how effective the motivator would be (or has been) for them. Circle your child's top five motivators (those that you numbered 1 to 5). Jot those five things down somewhere you can easily access, such as the notes section in your phone. Allow these areas of inspiration to help you encourage your child.

_____Board game/quality time with parent

_____Competitive nature

_____Creative supplies (new paint, canvas, gel pens)

_____Extra screen time (video game, tablet, etc.)

_____High five/fist bump

_____Later bedtime

_____Money

_____New book

_____Perfectionist/holds self to high standard

_____Piece of candy

_____Praise

_____Small prize from treasure box

_____Sticker

_____Sweet treat (cookie, ice cream, etc.)

_____Their choice of _____ (dinner, movie, etc.)

_____Time with extended family (grandparents, aunt, family friends)

_____Trip to the park

_____Trip to the store

_____Virtual money for video game

_____Wants to make others proud

How to Build Intrinsic Motivation

Everyone has their own set of intrinsic and extrinsic motivators. Intrinsic means it comes naturally so this type of motivation comes from within. Our internal motivators typically have to do with personality, upbringing, and mindset. A child who is naturally good at academics and enjoys the praise following their classroom achievements may be motivated by their thoughts of succeeding. This intrinsic motivator instills positive thoughts, which encourages more positive work habits. Another way that children can be naturally motivated is through desirable activities. When completing a task or assignment feels enjoyable, the fun reinforces the success. Parents play a large role in this process and can be a significant contributor to their child's intrinsic motivation in a variety of ways. Children not only crave fun, but they also need to feel valued. Be observant and compassionate of your child's needs. As their interests evolve, be ready and willing to evolve with them. Offer your child frequent praise and positivity, and they will naturally adapt this style of thinking for themselves. Over time, you may notice that your child has a healthier sense of self-confidence, leading to more natural motivation and less need for external rewards.

Have Open Discussions about What Your Child Loves

Taking the time out of your busy schedule to sit with your child and explore their thoughts and feelings is an important part of being an effective parent. Typically, parents know their child well enough to understand the things they like. But interests can change quickly, and heart-to-heart conversations are good for the soul. Try asking your child for an update. Ask them about their favorite things, career goals, and dreams for the future. You may be surprised at how much you didn't know.

Affirm Your Child's Strengths

Young children at this age are highly impressionable little humans. They are constantly taking in information from their world and applying it to their own life. This brings me to an important idea in parenting that says the way a parent speaks to their child becomes the child's inner voice. When a child is consistently praised for their strengths and abilities, those beliefs are eventually adopted as their own.

For a child to develop an internal sense of motivation, they must first believe that their efforts will be successful. Simply having a positive belief system can make a powerful difference in the way a child learns and performs.

Respect Your Child's Autonomy

Part of what makes parenting so difficult is finding the right balance between offering support and space. Allowing your child the ability to grow their autonomy, or independence, is an integral part of their development. This is especially true when it comes to executive functioning skills. Although it's important for the parent to help their child build that foundation, it's ultimately up to the child to use their skills effectively. Try to offer your child enough autonomy to solve their own problems, even if that means they make a few mistakes. You can always step in to help if they need it.

What You'll Need to Get Started

An important first step when starting something new with your child is to offer an age-appropriate introduction and identify a few goals. Offer clear and concrete expectations and allow your child to ask questions. It's common for children to feel overwhelmed or anxious when it comes to change, so helping them know what to expect can help ease some of that discomfort. Depending on your child's age and needs, they may appreciate some unstructured time to look through this workbook on their own. For younger children, it may be better to sit down with them and introduce the book before beginning the first activity. Keep an open mind and try not to set too many limits for your child while working through the strategies. The goal is to set your child up for success, so find a rhythm, a space, and a strategy that works for you both and stick with it. Be sure to create a consistent routine where you are dedicating time each day to working with your child on these skills. Even on the busier days, a short game or activity can make a difference. Try to gather all your materials prior to beginning to avoid wasting precious minutes and losing your child's interest. Here are the things you will need: crayons (or something to color with), a pencil, scissors, glue, and paper. At times, certain games or activities may require additional items; however, these should be things that you already have on hand.

HOW TO WORK WITH YOUR CHILD'S TEACHER

When it comes to your child, there are probably very few people who know them as well as you do. One of those few people is likely their teacher. Children spend hours in the classroom while using many of their executive function skills. Your child's teacher is probably aware of any issues with their social, emotional, or cognitive skills. Establish a working relationship with your child's teacher as early in the year as possible and communicate your concerns as they arise. Sometimes issues at home can be circumstantial and specific to the family dynamic. Other times negative behaviors at home are congruent with classroom issues that the teacher may be struggling with as well. Some of the most common issues that affect children in the school setting stem from delayed executive function skills. Either way, it's vital that parents and teachers be able to work together and find effective solutions for classroom issues. If your child seems to be having persistent classroom or academic difficulties, it may be time to schedule a meeting with the school. Often referred to as an "S-team" meeting or "IEP meeting," this is typically the first step in obtaining accommodations or an individualized education program (IEP) for your child. This meeting takes place at the school and includes all the teachers and administrators who play a role in your child's education. During the meeting, concerns will be discussed and goals will be formed. A plan will be created providing effective strategies that will be used to help your child achieve academic success.

Key Takeaways

Offering frequent words of encouragement can have a significant positive impact on the ability to learn and apply new skills. It's important to remember that your child is a person and to treat them with the same respect as you would anyone else. Be patient and flexible and allow them enough independence for trial and error. Prioritizing the nourishment of your own mental health will ensure your readiness to nurture your child's emotional needs.

- Your child wants to meet your expectations, and they want to make you proud.
- Use the proper terminology or diagnosis when discussing your child's challenges.
- Maintaining a more positive and compassionate mindset will encourage your child to stay positive and offer themselves compassion, too.
- Although consequences can be effective and necessary at times, studies have shown that positive reinforcement is the best approach for children with executive function difficulties.
- Fun is the key ingredient to keeping your child engaged and interested.

PART II

EXECUTIVE FUNCTIONING GAMES AND ACTIVITIES

Now it's time for some interactive learning and fun! The next eight chapters are full of games and activities that will keep your child entertained while exercising their executive skills. The chapters are arranged according to the typical sequence of executive skill development during childhood. Feel free to roam around the chapters, games, and activities in a way that best suits your child. Remember that the exercises range from beginner to advanced, to offer practice for children with a wide range of abilities and skill sets. Also, please keep in mind that the executive skills in the later chapters typically develop later in childhood and may be too advanced for younger children.

CHAPTER 3

Master Your Impulses

Having the ability to stop and think before we act is an executive skill called "impulse control." This is the underlying skill that enables a child to maintain safe behaviors, healthy boundaries, and age-appropriate expectations. In this chapter, you will help your child sharpen their impulse control through games and activities that require slowing down and thinking things through. You may notice that some of the games seem familiar as many classic childhood games are an exercise in self-control. By practicing these skills, your child will learn the art of mindfulness and gain a better sense of self-awareness.

BUILDING IMPULSE CONTROL

I began working with a little boy named Jacob when he was eight years old. Jacob was adopted by his family when he was three years old, but unfortunately endured extensive physical abuse and neglect while in the care of his biological mother. Jacob's adoptive parents came to me with complaints that he was defiant and moody at home and having difficulty paying attention at school. Jacob's teacher would often report that he would socialize during class, disrupt instructional time, and lacked empathy toward classmates. Meanwhile, Jacob always maintained exceptional grades. After further assessment and clinical observation, Jacob was diagnosed with reactive attachment disorder (RAD). As the name states, children with this disorder are often emotionally reactive and struggle with impulse control. For Jacob, the combination of early childhood trauma and underfunctioning executive skills was making it difficult to follow rules and maintain healthy relationships. Jacob participated in trauma-focused cognitive behavioral therapy (TF-CBT) with elements of play therapy. He was able to practice self-control through fun activities and games during sessions that improved his self-control outside of the therapy setting. Although Jacob's condition is chronic and he will likely experience lifelong difficulties, creating an early awareness and practice of his impulsive tendencies is a foundation that he can continue to build on.

Everyday Strategies to Build Impulse Control

Impulse control is a frequent struggle for most parents, those moments when their child pushes a boundary or seems to purposefully defy a rule. This is when your self-control becomes crucial. How helpful would it be for the parent to respond to their child with anger? Most parents understand that this isn't the way to be effective.

Instead, healthy strategies for coping are set into place when parents use their fully formed prefrontal cortex to maintain control of their actions. This is one of the many ways that parents model impulse control for their children. Although it's great to have structured activities for practicing executive skills, it's unrealistic to think that children can only benefit from organized learning. The reality is our daily lives offer plenty of opportunities to display effective self-control.

- When you use self-control yourself, point it out to your child.
- When you observe them using this skill, praise them for staying in control.
- Normalize moments of your own temptation and allow your child to see you work through a challenge.
- Be mindful of the times when you act impulsively and offer honest communication about skills you are working to improve. Accepting and admitting your mistakes shows your child that even parents can be a work in progress.

WAIT IT OUT

Get ready for the ultimate test of your child's self-control! In this activity, your child will master the art of patience as they wait for your return to enjoy a treat.

GOOD FOR: Impulse Control, Following Directions, Emotional Regulation

MATERIALS:

A treat that your child loves (candy, marshmallows, crackers, etc.)

TIME NEEDED: 5 minutes

HELPFUL TIP:

It may be difficult for your child to sit and wait. If you return to find them playing, fidgeting, or anywhere but sitting at the table, that's okay! In this situation, occupying themselves was likely the key to their success.

INSTRUCTIONS:

1. Introduce the activity to your child by saying, "I have a really fun activity for us, and you will earn a treat at the end."
2. Have your child sit at a table.
3. Sit the treat on the table in front of them. Instruct them that they may *not* eat it until you return. Sympathize with "I know it's hard to wait, but I will be right back."
4. Walk away for about 3 minutes. (Be sure to stay accountable here—set a timer if you need to.)
5. Return to sit with your child.
6. If your child listened, give them enthusiastic praise: "Great job waiting. Enjoy!"
7. If your child did not listen, remain calm and validate: "That was a difficult request."

LET'S TALK ABOUT IT!

If they listened: "What helped you stay in control and avoid eating your treat?"

If they didn't listen: "What could have helped you stay in control to avoid eating your treat?"

If they left the table: "I know sometimes it's hard to sit and be patient. Why didn't you stay at the table?"

SLEEPY SLOTH, BOUNCING BUNNY

In this unique version of red light, green light, your child will practice slowing down to control their impulses with a specific external cue.

GOOD FOR: Impulse Control

MATERIALS:

None

TIME NEEDED: 10 minutes

HELPFUL TIP:
Have fun and get creative with this game! Invite friends and family members to join in. Improvise by adding more animal behaviors like a slithering snake or frozen fox.

INSTRUCTIONS:

1. Prepare your child for the game by saying, "We're going to play a fun game called "Sleepy Sloth, Bouncing Bunny!"
2. Demonstrate that a sleepy sloth will find a cozy place to curl up and nap (lie on the floor very still).
3. Demonstrate that a bouncing bunny will jump up to bounce around like this (hop, jump, bounce).
4. Begin the game by being bouncing bunnies. Jump around and have fun with your child.
5. After one or two minutes of jumping, switch to sleepy sloths. Lie down with your child and model curling up for a nap.
6. Continue alternating between the two for several rounds.

LET'S TALK ABOUT IT!

"Did you notice how you needed to take deep breaths to help your body slow down?"

FREEZE DANCE

This classic game is one that almost every child loves, and it's a perfect way to practice impulse control. Grab the kids, adults, and even the pets, and get ready to dance!

GOOD FOR: Impulse Control, Flexibility

MATERIALS:

Music that can be paused
Phone or something to play music on

TIME NEEDED:
10 minutes

HELPFUL TIP:
You can spice up this game by naming a specific dance move each time the music returns (twirl, leap, dab).

INSTRUCTIONS:

1. Introduce this game by asking your child if they feel up to a game of freeze dance. If they know the game already, skip to step 3.
2. Explain that this game requires dancing to the music. When the music stops, everyone freezes!
3. Invite your child to choose the song/music.
4. Grab some tunes and start dancing.
5. After a few minutes, sneak over and pause the music. You may even yell "FREEZE!"
6. Everyone must stop dancing exactly where they are and pretend to be frozen.
7. Resume the music and continue to boogie.
8. Continue this cycle until the song ends (or whenever feels comfortable).

LET'S TALK ABOUT IT!

"What was your favorite part about this game?"
"What was your least favorite part about this game?"

WHACK THE AVOCADO

This silly and interactive game brings fun and foundational executive skills together.

GOOD FOR: Impulse Control

MATERIALS:

Stack of index cards
Crayons

TIME NEEDED:
10 minutes

HELPFUL TIP:
For an added challenge, increase the speed that you discard. You could also try incorporating new rules, such as using only their left hand or having your child shout "Avocado!" instead of whacking it.

INSTRUCTIONS:

1. Begin by helping your child draw "avocados" on eight of the index cards. These do not need to be perfect—a green circle will do just fine.
2. Mix up the avocado cards with the blank cards and tell your child that as you lay the cards down, they should watch for the avocado.
3. Tell them when they see it, whack the avocado! Avoid smacking the blank cards.
4. Hold the stack of cards facing down and slowly place them one by one on the table, picture facing up.
5. Continue the game until you're out of cards.

LET'S TALK ABOUT IT!

"What helped you avoid whacking the wrong card?" Discuss with your child what you noticed: "I noticed that you kept your hand farther away from the cards so you wouldn't accidently whack the wrong card."

GROCERY GRAB

In this fast-paced game, your child will race against the clock while using self-control to grab the correct items from the grocery list.

GOOD FOR: Impulse Control, Working Memory, Planning and Prioritization

MATERIALS:

Items that are stocked in your kitchen
Plastic grocery bag (or any empty container)
Timer/clock

TIME NEEDED:
10 minutes

HELPFUL TIP:
You may need to help your child navigate to find the items. Bring the game to life by "ringing up" the items for purchase.

INSTRUCTIONS:

1. Pretend that you're sending your child to the store (in the kitchen) to pick up some things.
2. Tell them the store is closing soon.
3. Create a short list of items that are in your kitchen pantry, cabinets, or drawers.
4. Set a timer for 5 minutes.
5. On your count, your child begins searching for the items and adding them to their bag as you shout out the items on the list (two apples, three gummy snacks, one carrot).
6. Your child wins the game when they get everything on the list before the time runs out.

LET'S TALK ABOUT IT!

> "Was it easier or harder knowing you were under a time limit?"

STACKS OF SNACKS

A lunchroom favorite, this activity is a delicious way to satisfy their after-school hunger while practicing their impulse control skills!

GOOD FOR: Impulse Control, Organization, Problem-Solving

MATERIALS:

Stackable foods (crackers, cookies, cheese, pepperoni)
Plate

TIME NEEDED:
5 minutes

HELPFUL TIP:
Try this activity when your child is hungry for an extra challenge.

INSTRUCTIONS:

1. Help your child choose a delicious and nutritious snack for both of you that is somewhat flat and stackable.
2. Sit down at a table with your child and say it's time to play with some food.
3. Invite your child to build towers, create castles, or come up with their own ideas of things to build with their snack.
4. Play along with your food, too!
5. Continue this activity until you run out of building materials (and you're no longer hungry).

LET'S TALK ABOUT IT!

"What's your favorite food to stack?"

DON'T SAY IT!

Grab your child's favorite rhyming book and find a cozy spot to read. In this activity, your child will practice their reading skills while working to control their impulses.

GOOD FOR: Impulse Control, Working Memory

MATERIALS:

Children's book on your child's reading level

TIME NEEDED:
5 minutes

HELPFUL TIP:
Grow the audience and enjoy this shared! Invite siblings, friends, and pets to listen to the story.

INSTRUCTIONS:

1. First, have your child choose a favorite book to read. Ideally, the book will have repetitive rhyming words.
2. Pick a word that shows up often in the book and tell your child that word is off-limits. "Don't say it!"
3. Read the story to your child first to model skipping the chosen word.
4. Once you finish the story, pass the book to your child and say, "Your turn!" Have them read the story to you, ensuring that they are avoiding the chosen word.

LET'S TALK ABOUT IT!

> "As you were reading the story, you paused to avoid blurting out that one word." Talk about how we can pause to carefully respond in other things as well.

ON THE PAGE ACTIVITY

COLOR CODE

A great way to challenge our impulse control is to give our brain a task that requires extra time to process. In this fill-in-the-blank activity, your child will need to follow the instructions carefully.

INSTRUCTIONS:

1. Take a look with your child at the following words.
2. Notice how many of the words and colors do not match.
3. Instruct your child to circle the words using the correct color that the word says. (The word says "blue" but the letters are red, so the child circles the word in blue.)
4. Clarify that your child should focus on the word, not its color.

BLUE RED GREEN YELLOW

PURPLE ORANGE BROWN PINK

HELPFUL TIP: If your child is struggling with this activity or needs additional help, suggest that they read the word out loud. This may help them remember the color more easily.

LET'S TALK ABOUT IT!

"What was your strategy for this activity?"

BALANCE THE BUTTERFLY

In this mindfulness game, your child will practice impulse control by slowing down their mind and body.

GOOD FOR: Impulse Control, Emotional Control

MATERIALS:

Paper
Crayons
Scissors

TIME NEEDED:
15 minutes

HELPFUL TIP:
For an added challenge, try balancing the butterfly on one finger, your head, or on your nose.

INSTRUCTIONS:

1. Introduce the game by asking, "Is it possible to catch a butterfly?" Encourage your child to describe in detail what catching a butterfly would entail. ("Should you move around or be still like a statue?")
2. Help them draw a butterfly (about the size of their hand) on their paper. Invite them to color and add details to their butterfly, then cut it out.
3. Now the fun part! Challenge your child to balance the butterfly in the palm of their hand while you count.
4. Now it's your turn to balance it while your child counts. (Other family members/friends can join, too.)
5. Whoever can balance the butterfly without dropping it for the longest amount of time wins!

LET'S TALK ABOUT IT!

> "What are some other times when it would be helpful to slow down and be mindful of our body?"

SAME, SAME, DIFFERENT

Sometimes our words come out before our brains have time to think. In this game of stop and think, your child will use their impulse control skills to avoid blurting out the wrong word.

GOOD FOR: Impulse Control, Working Memory

MATERIALS:

10 index cards
Pencil

TIME NEEDED:
10 minutes

HELPFUL TIP:
No matter the child's age, this activity is meant to be challenging. Go slow and give prompts as needed to help them get started. You may need to play a few rounds before they get the hang of it.

INSTRUCTIONS:

1. First, you will need to write down ten different words on separate index cards. Choose words that have opposites (up, down, over, under, right, left, forward, backward).
2. Explain to your child that sometimes our brains work so fast that we blurt out words by mistake, and this game will help them practice slowing down.
3. You will begin by slowly showing your child a card as you say "same." Tell them to read the word.
4. For the third card, say "different" and ask them to say the opposite word.
5. Speed up the game and continue the trend of same, same, different.
6. Take turns to see who can make the fewest mistakes.

LET'S TALK ABOUT IT!

> "What are some other times you have been tempted to blurt out the first thing that comes to mind?"

MINDFUL MOUNTAIN

A fantastic way to exercise self-control is through the practice of mindfulness, which helps us acknowledge thoughts and feelings without judgment. In this activity, your child will use mindful thinking to practice controlling their thoughts.

GOOD FOR: Impulse Control

MATERIALS:

None

TIME NEEDED:
10 minutes

HELPFUL TIP:
Mindfulness practice should be calm and relaxing. Invite your child to breathe deeply through their nose and out through their mouth throughout this exercise.

LET'S TALK ABOUT IT!

"What did you notice as we were doing this mindfulness exercise?"

INSTRUCTIONS:

1. For this activity, you'll want to find a space that is quiet with few distractions.
2. Find a comfortable seated position for both you and your child.
3. Explain to your child that mindfulness is how we can acknowledge our thoughts ("Hello!") and let them pass by.
4. Compare being mindful to being a mountain. The mountain isn't worried about the people who may climb it, or the cars that may drive up it, or the animals that may pass over it. The mountain is just the mountain.
5. Invite your child to imagine they are a mountain. Have them lower their gaze or close their eyes.
6. Slowly identify various people and things that are passing over the mountain. Imagining the activity on their mountain will help them stay in the moment.
7. Remind your child to be patient with themselves. Reassure them that their thoughts may wander away, and they can gently guide them back.
8. After several minutes, have them open their eyes or come back to the present moment.

SELF-CONTROL SUPERPOWERS

It can be helpful for children to reflect on moments of success. This not only helps build their confidence but also helps them review the effective application of their skills. In this activity, your child will identify times when they used their self-control superpower.

GOOD FOR: Impulse Control, Working Memory

MATERIALS:

Piece of paper
Pencil

TIME NEEDED:
10 minutes

HELPFUL TIP:
For additional practice, invite your child to role-play one of their examples. Have them identify when they are practicing self-control.

INSTRUCTIONS:

1. Have your child draw four large circles on their paper.
2. Ask your child to think about times when they have held back from saying something unkind, chosen a more nutritious food, paused before acting, etc.
3. Have your child briefly explain a time they used self-control in each of the circles.
4. Invite your child to choose one to tell you about (if they feel comfortable).
5. Praise your child for this accomplishment!

LET'S TALK ABOUT IT!

> "What makes self-control easier? What makes self-control more difficult?"

Key Takeaways

Impulse control is often one of the first executive skills to develop that will continue to strengthen over time. Try to remain patient with your child and model your own impulse control skills. Refer to this section of the book anytime you feel your child needs a review.

- Having the ability to stop and think before we act is an executive skill called "impulse control."
- Be mindful of the times when you act impulsively and offer honest communication about skills you are working to improve.
- Normalize moments of your own temptation and allow your child to see you work through a challenge.
- By practicing these skills, your child will learn the art of mindfulness and gain a better sense of self-awareness.

CHAPTER 4

Make Your Memory Work for You

Anytime we learn something new, it requires us to use working memory. Without it, you wouldn't be able to build and store the library of information needed to understand these new concepts. Working memory is the part of our short-term memory that allows us to process information, temporarily store those details, and use the information as needed. Children who lack this skill may face difficulties in the classroom and elsewhere. As with all executive skills, children gradually strengthen their working memory with age and practice. In this chapter, you will be guided through a variety of games and activities uniquely created to help your child hold on to details while completing a task.

WORKING MEMORY OVERLOAD

Blake was a six-year-old boy who was brought to therapy to improve his coping skills. Blake was involved in various sports and excelled as an athlete. He came from a long line of athletes, including some who had successfully made it to the professional level. When I met with Blake's parents, their love for their son radiated in the room. They spoke at length about his early development of milestones and vibrant personality. They were extremely proud of his achievements. As I spent more time with Blake, I discovered that he had high expectations for himself that were unrealistic and had often originated from his parents.

Blake desperately wanted to be "just as good" as the older players on the team, especially since his coach and his parents talked about his skills being as good as theirs. No matter how much he practiced, he found that it was difficult to keep up with the more advanced players on his team. There was simply too much to remember, which was overloading his working memory and his self-esteem. As Blake was stretched beyond his capabilities, he became frustrated and overwhelmed. His parents attended a few sessions to learn more about executive functioning and better understand the challenges their child was facing. They were able to determine that the level of expectations for Blake were too advanced for his development. By making a few modifications at home and incorporating practice for his working memory and emotion regulation in therapy, Blake was able to return to his love of sports with the skills he needed to be successful.

Everyday Strategies to Improve Working Memory

Believe it or not, you have already begun teaching your child the skill of working memory. At the grocery store, as you clean the house, and while cooking dinner, your child has observed this executive skill in action. The beautiful thing about parenting is that you subconsciously model these important skills for your child. Now you can start to incorporate your child into the task.

For example, give them the role of list manager at the grocery store and have them check off items as you go. When the time comes for your child to clean their room, help them keep a mental checklist by offering prompts, such as "your bed is made, now let's pick up your dirty clothes." Another great way to strengthen their working memory is to teach your child a new hobby. Think of something new they would enjoy and teach it to them. As they follow your step-by-step instructions, they'll use their working memory to recall what they're learning and apply it to practice and master the skill. As your child grows, so will their capabilities. By encouraging your child to participate in these exercises, you will not only be spending valuable time with them, but you will be cultivating an essential skill for their future achievements.

COLOR MY HOUSE

In this activity, your child will use their working memory as they listen and follow your directions.

GOOD FOR: Working Memory, Following Directions

MATERIALS:

Paper
Pencil
Crayons
Art materials such as glue, glitter, feathers, pom-poms, etc. (optional)

TIME NEEDED:
10 minutes

HELPFUL TIP:
For an added challenge, try giving your child multistep instructions, such as "color the ______ blue, then color the ______ green."

INSTRUCTIONS:

1. Begin by drawing a picture of a house. Be sure to include at least a few details, such as a door, windows, and a roof.
2. Give your child the picture along with the materials.
3. Give them detailed instructions for coloring or decorating the house. ("Color the window to the right yellow," "Color the roof blue," or "Add polka dots to the door.")
4. Continue instructing your child until they have decorated the entire house.

LET'S TALK ABOUT IT!

"You really had to pay close attention to my instructions and remember the details. What other times do you need to listen closely and remember details?"

FOLLOW ME!

This version of follow the leader helps children strengthen their working memory skills while having fun.

GOOD FOR: Following Directions, Turn-Taking, Working Memory

MATERIALS:

None

TIME NEEDED:
10 minutes

HELPFUL TIP:
For added fun, you could try this activity to music, take it outside, or use musical instruments. Challenge your child by giving two or three directions at a time. If they can easily keep up, add more.

INSTRUCTIONS:

1. Invite your child to a game of Follow the Leader.
2. Have your child line up behind you and follow your sequence of moves. ("March and clap your hands!" or "Hop, then turn around.")
3. Lead them around the house while they follow your commands.
4. Now it's time to switch roles! Have your child take the leader role and you follow them.

LET'S TALK ABOUT IT!

> "What if I would have only told you the movements to do? Would this game have been harder?"

MAKE IT MATCH

In this familiar children's game, your child will use their working memory to make card matches.

GOOD FOR: Working Memory, Emotional Control, Sustained Attention and Goal-Oriented Persistence

MATERIALS:

Construction paper (or any paper)
Pencil/crayons
Stickers (optional)
Scissors

TIME NEEDED:
15 minutes

HELPFUL TIPS:

If your child quickly loses interest, move to a different activity and try having the game prepared to play next time.

Teach your child to slowly study the cards before turning them back over to help them retain the memory.

LET'S TALK ABOUT IT!

"Sometimes it's hard to remember where we last saw something. What was the trick that I taught you to help you remember?"

INSTRUCTIONS:

1. Help your child make their own cards: Using the paper and pencil, draw two horizontal lines across and three vertical lines down to create twelve squares.
2. Have your child choose six images (such as animals, food, toys) and help them draw them or place stickers, on two cards each. Remember that each card should have a match.
3. Invite your child to be as simple or creative as they want.
4. Once they have completed the drawings, help them cut out the cards.
5. Now you're ready to play the game! Simply arrange the cards in a few rows, pictures facing down.
6. Take turns flipping two of the cards over to see if they match. If the cards match, the player gets to keep those cards. If they don't match, the player flips them back over and it's the next player's turn.
7. The game continues until all the matches are found. The player with the most pairs wins!

WHAT DO YOU SEE?

Your child is sure to love this game of Now You See It, Now You Don't! In this exercise, your child will practice using their working memory as they attempt to remember things they can no longer see.

GOOD FOR: Working Memory, Attention to Detail

MATERIALS:

Any item that can easily be hidden

A blanket or towel to hide the object (optional)

TIME NEEDED: 10 minutes

HELPFUL TIP:
Some children may need to first practice describing object details while they are looking at them. Teach your child to say the details out loud to help with memory retention.

INSTRUCTIONS:

1. Begin the game by having your child sit with a table in front of them.
2. Take one of the objects and sit it on the table for 3 seconds.
3. Ask your child, "What do you see? I'll count to three. One . . . Two . . . Three."
4. Hide the object behind your back or under the blanket.
5. Ask your child a detail about the object ("What color was it?" "Was it bumpy or soft?").
6. Challenge your child to correctly identify each object without looking.

LET'S TALK ABOUT IT!

"What are some of the objects that we used in the game? Did it help when you described them out loud, or what helped you remember?"

DOUGH MUCH FUN!

Did you know that it requires working memory for us to follow a recipe? In this fun and creative activity, your child will use this skill to create their own playdough.

GOOD FOR: Working Memory, Impulse Control

MATERIALS:

2 bowls
½ cup flour, plus more for the work surface
2 tablespoons table salt
¼ cup water
1 tablespoon vegetable oil
Food coloring or colorful drink mix (optional)
Plastic sandwich bag

TIME NEEDED:
15 minutes

HELPFUL TIP:
Assume that this activity will get messy. Try to allow yourself plenty of time and space to enjoy the creative process!

INSTRUCTIONS:

Begin by setting clear expectations for your child's role in this activity. Tell them to wait for your instruction. ("You are going to be in charge of mixing. Here is your spoon. I will let you know when it's time to mix.") Now it's time to make the playdough!

1. Combine the flour and salt in a bowl.
2. In a separate bowl, combine the water and oil (if using, add a few drops of your food coloring to this mixture).
3. Pour the liquid mixture into the dry mixture.
4. Sprinkle a little flour onto your work surface and begin kneading the dough with your hands (allow your child to do this part if they prefer).
5. Store the playdough in a plastic sandwich bag in the refrigerator.

LET'S TALK ABOUT IT!

> "When we are following a recipe, it's important that we do the steps in the correct order. What can happen if we do the steps out of order?"

FINISH THE STORY

In this activity, your child will use their working memory to add a unique ending to a familiar story.

GOOD FOR: Working Memory, Imagination

MATERIALS:

A short children's book
Plain paper
Pencil or crayons

TIME NEEDED:
10 minutes

HELPFUL TIP:
Try to avoid prompting or rereading the story to your child. If they ask for help, encourage them to use what they can remember.

INSTRUCTIONS:

1. Begin by explaining to your child that you're going to tell them a familiar story, and you need their help to give the story a new ending.
2. Choose an age-appropriate short story to tell. You may read from a book or tell the story from memory. Remember not to tell the entire story.
3. Near the end, pause and ask your child to draw a picture of how the story could end. Invite them to use their imagination and add new details that aren't usually included in the story.
4. Have them retell the story in their own words, using their newly reimagined conclusion.

LET'S TALK ABOUT IT!

> "As you were adding the new ending, what helped you remember the details?"

MEMORY TREASURE HUNT

Searching for treasure is always a great adventure! In this activity, your child will practice using their working memory to find a hidden surprise.

GOOD FOR: Working Memory, Problem-Solving

MATERIALS:

Paper
Pencil
An object to hide

TIME NEEDED:
15 minutes

HELPFUL TIP:
Have fun with this exercise! Decorate the house, play pirate/adventure music, make props, etc. Remember, fun is the key ingredient to helping your child learn.

INSTRUCTIONS:

1. Before you begin, you will need to draw a simple treasure map. Write down directions, such as "go up the stairs" and "turn left at the lamp." The final direction should lead your child to the hidden object.
2. Tell your child that you have set up a treasure hunt with a hidden treasure somewhere in the house.
3. Give them the map and instruct them to follow it to find the hidden treasure.
4. Try to give them some space to work through this exercise independently.
5. Be sure to celebrate their achievement when they locate the object!

LET'S TALK ABOUT IT!

"Was it ever difficult to focus being inside with the many different distractions?"

"What could have made the map better?"

SPELL IT OUT

Get ready for another fun-filled exercise for strengthening working memory! Similar to the game of HORSE, this exercise will have your child copying your moves and shooting for goals.

GOOD FOR: Working Memory, Frustration Tolerance

MATERIALS:

Ball or paper
Laundry basket

TIME NEEDED:
10 minutes

HELPFUL TIP:
For added difficulty, use mental notes for keeping track of each player's letters instead of writing them down. Invite the whole family to play—this game is even more fun with a group of people!

INSTRUCTIONS:

1. First, you will need to set up the game in an open area (or outside).
2. Instruct your child to create a medium-size paper wad if they don't have a ball.
3. Have your child choose a word to spell out (seven letters or less) or use their name.
4. To start the game, toss the ball into the basket.
5. When someone makes a basket, the other player must copy the exact shot in the same way from the same spot. Spin, jump, or sing silly songs. Anything goes!
6. If they make it in the basket, then they get a turn to create their own move.
7. Anytime a player misses the shot they attempt to copy, they add a letter from the chosen word.
8. The first player to receive all the letters in the word loses the game.

LET'S TALK ABOUT IT!

"Even something as simple as a letter can be hard to remember when we are multitasking."

"Do you think it's helpful for us to write things down to help us remember?"

GUESS WHAT I'M THINKING

In this version of the guessing game, your child will practice using their working memory skills as they attempt to identify what you're thinking of.

GOOD FOR: Problem-Solving, Working Memory, Impulse Control

MATERIALS:

None

TIME NEEDED:
5 minutes

HELPFUL TIP:
Try not to give your child prompts or additional information. This exercise is most effective when they can keep a mental list of the details. During your turn, model how to keep mental notes by verbally recapping the details as you go.

INSTRUCTIONS:

1. Begin by saying, "Guess what I'm thinking of."
2. Name the category that it would belong to: animal, food, or object ("It's a type of animal").
3. Instruct them to ask yes or no questions to get more information. ("Does it have fur?" "Does it live in the ocean?" "Can we have it as a pet?")
4. Each player gets three chances to correctly guess the thing.
5. Switch roles in the game. Have your child ask you the questions now.
6. Whoever can correctly identify three of the things wins the game!

LET'S TALK ABOUT IT!

> "Sometimes we receive a lot of information all at once. The details can swirl around in our brain and make us feel overwhelmed."
>
> "What can we do to help us remember?"

LET'S PLAN A PARTY!

Planning a party can be full of excitement and many important details! In this write-in activity, have your child match the items and materials needed to successfully throw a birthday party. If necessary, you can read the list to your child.

Birthday To-Do List:	Party Items and Materials:
Send invitations to guests	Streamers, birthday banner, and balloons
Order pizza	Bakery information
Order cupcakes	Phone number for pizzeria
Pick up supplies for face painting	Invitations, envelopes, and stamps
Make goodie bags	Paint and paintbrushes
Buy decorations	Wrapping paper/gift bags
Wrap presents	Treats and favors

LET'S TALK ABOUT IT!

> "Planning an event can be challenging, so what are some helpful ways to help our brain remember the details?"

MATH MEMORIZATION

One of the best ways to strengthen the skill of working memory is through practicing math. In this game, your child will need to remember a series of numbers to create and solve a problem.

GOOD FOR: Working Memory, Problem-Solving

MATERIALS:

Dice
Coin
Paper
Pencil

TIME NEEDED:
10 minutes

HELPFUL TIP:
If your child is strong in math, add a challenge by setting a timer and giving your child a limited amount of time to complete the problem.

INSTRUCTIONS:

1. Begin by setting up the game with the materials laid on the table.
2. Explain to your child that they will be setting up a math problem using the dice and coin.
3. They will roll the dice to get their numbers.
4. They will flip the coin to know whether to add or subtract, multiply or divide (heads = add/multiply, tails = subtract/divide).
5. Once they have set up the equation, ask them to solve it.
6. Continue the game and switch roles if your child prefers.

LET'S TALK ABOUT IT!

"I wonder if this game would have been easier if the equation had already been written out? What do you think?" Discuss the strategy of writing down details as you go.

GUESS THE MAGIC WORD

In this classic guessing game, your child will use their working memory to keep track of letters and attempt to guess a magic word.

GOOD FOR: Working Memory, Problem-Solving

MATERIALS:

Paper
Pencil

TIME NEEDED:
10 minutes

HELPFUL TIP:
You can increase the level of difficulty by using longer words. For a fun challenge, have the player be blindfolded or unable to see the paper.

INSTRUCTIONS:

1. Set up the game by choosing a short word (seven letters or less) to designate as the magic word.
2. Draw the corresponding number of blanks on the paper.
3. Let your child know that they are trying to guess the magic word and tell them how many letters are in the word.
4. As they guess the letters, you will add them to the correct blank or write them down with an "x" through them if they are not in the word.
5. Each time they guess incorrectly, a letter gets added to the word "magic."
6. To win the game, they will need to correctly identify the word before "magic" is spelled out.

LET'S TALK ABOUT IT!

> "We use working memory for a lot of things, including spelling. What other times at school do you need to remember a lot of details?"

LET'S GO ON VACATION

When it comes to packing a bag for a trip, it's important to know where you're going. Keep this in mind to ensure you take the appropriate items. For this activity, your child will use their working memory as they role-play packing their bags for an adventure!

GOOD FOR: Working Memory, Prioritizing and Planning, Organization

MATERIALS:

Backpack, luggage, or any type of bag
Personal items (in their current location)

TIME NEEDED:
15 minutes

HELPFUL TIP:
There are many ways to make this activity extra fun. Look up the current weather conditions for that area. Research upcoming events or cultural celebrations. Consider going the extra step to set up their "dream vacation" at home.

INSTRUCTIONS:

1. Begin the activity by allowing your child to pick their dream vacation!
2. Explain that you are going to pretend that you're going there.
3. Discuss the important details of the trip (climate, activities, length of stay) and some ideas of what to pack.
4. It's time to get going! Have your child role-play packing their bag for vacation.
5. Allow them some time and space to work independently.
6. Follow up with them after about 10 minutes. Review the items they included in their bag and discuss what else they may have needed.
7. Praise their hard work!

LET'S TALK ABOUT IT!

> "There were a lot of details to remember in this activity. Was the information easier to remember since you were excited thinking about the trip?"

Key Takeaways

Working memory plays an important role in many of our day-to-day tasks. Without it, we would lack the ability to complete multiple-step tasks such as household chores. For children, working memory enables them to be successful in both the home and school environments. From cleaning their room to playing a sport to completing a math test, kids require this essential executive skill to help them reach their best self. It's not only a matter of childhood success, it's a matter of adulthood fulfillment.

- Anytime we learn something new, we require the skill of working memory.
- As with all executive skills, children gradually strengthen their working memory with age and practice.
- The beautiful thing about parenting is that so much of what you do is modeling an important skill for your child.
- By encouraging your child to participate in these daily activities, you will not only be spending valuable time with them, but you will be cultivating an essential skill for their future achievements.

CHAPTER 5

Manage Your Emotions

Emotions are an essential part of the human experience. These feelings add zest to our life and allow us to connect deeply with those around us. So why do they sometimes cause problems? The challenge with emotions is not that we feel them—it's how we choose to manage them. This is especially true when it comes to parenting. Control your emotions and you will provide your child with a healthy example that lasts a lifetime. It will also promote a healthy parent–child relationship. In this chapter, your child will gain important, effective emotion management skills and strategies through fun and engaging games and activities.

BIG EMOTIONS CAUSING BIG PROBLEMS

Addison was a four-year-old girl who was referred to therapy by her pediatrician. Addison's dad and stepmom said she was starting to act out and they wanted to address any issues early on. After meeting with both sets of Addison's parents, I was pleased by their healthy coparenting relationship. I learned that they had divorced when she was two years old, and the separate households took great care in providing a nurturing environment for Addison. It had taken both parents by surprise when she began to behave differently.

At home, Addison would become easily frustrated by challenging tasks, which caused meltdowns. The reports from her preschool teacher were similar. During non-preferred or difficult tasks, Addison would start "shutting down" and become tearful. Addison began participating in weekly play therapy and learning age-appropriate strategies for regulating her emotions. Addison's parents attended separate sessions to build their understanding of normal childhood development and learn effective strategies to support their daughter at home. After consistent practice during and outside sessions, she was able to improve her ability to cope with the big feelings that she was experiencing. Addison didn't want to behave badly; she just simply needed the words and skills to better manage her emotions.

Everyday Strategies to Build Emotional Control

A common misconception about children is that they misbehave to be mean. In other words, kids who act bad are bad kids. This belief is completely false and can actually cause negative behaviors to increase! The truth is children are still learning how to control their emotions and are looking to their parents for inspiration.

Consider a time when your child has been upset or overwhelmed. How did you respond? Let's be honest, sometimes it's tough to stay calm, especially when it's the end of the day and everyone is tired. Just remember, you can't fight fire with fire. Learning to manage your own emotions is incredibly important for your own mental health, as well as your child's. When emotional control is consistently practiced in the home, your child will pick up on those healthy habits.

Try using strategies such as deep breathing or taking a time-out during a disagreement. Keep an open dialogue and try to help your child identify their own emotions as they surface. You would be surprised at just how well they can communicate their feelings when they are given the words and supportive space to do so. Finally, be honest with yourself. If your emotions are frequently causing issues in your daily life, speak to a professional if you can or seek out someone you trust who can listen and offer support. One of the greatest gifts you can offer your child is the gift of an emotionally healthy parent.

FEELINGS FACES

In this fun and creative activity, your child will develop foundational skills of emotional awareness through creating faces with feeling.

GOOD FOR: Emotional Control

MATERIALS:

Paper
Pencil
Art supplies (playdough, dry macaroni, pom-poms)

TIME NEEDED:
10 minutes

HELPFUL TIP:
If your child is unsure of how the emotion should look, you may need to provide an example through images on your phone or even showing them with your facial expressions.

INSTRUCTIONS:

1. Draw a large circle on two separate pieces of paper.
2. Tell your child that you both will create feelings faces with their materials.
3. Lay out the materials you will use.
4. Take turns picking an emotion and creating it on your paper (Use pieces of the dough to create the eyes, nose, and mouth that reflect the emotion).
5. Once the face is complete, discuss the emotion with your child (experience with the feeling, how it feels in your body, what you do when you feel that way).
6. Clear the paper and start over with a different feeling.
7. Continue this activity for as long as your child will tolerate it. Do multiple sessions if you need to. Try to at least review faces that are happy, sad, mad, and scared.

LET'S TALK ABOUT IT!

"Show me with your face which feeling was your favorite!" (Try to guess the feeling based on their expression, or explore a time when they felt that emotion.)

ACTING ON EMOTION

In this silly acting game, your child will continue building their understanding of emotions and begin to connect feelings to behaviors.

GOOD FOR: Emotional Control, Impulse Control

MATERIALS:

Paper
Pencil
Scissors
Timer

TIME NEEDED:
15 minutes

HELPFUL TIP:
Use props to act out the feeling for added fun (umbrella to symbolize rain for sad, pillow to represent sleep for tired).

INSTRUCTIONS:

1. Begin by writing down a variety of age-appropriate feeling words (4 to 6 feelings) with simple corresponding faces beneath the word.
2. Cut out each feeling and fold them up. Make a pile of them on the table.
3. Choose a feeling and set the timer for 3 minutes.
4. Use facial expressions and movements to act out the emotion.
5. The other player tries to correctly identify the feeling.
6. Take turns choosing and acting out a feeling until all the folded papers are gone.

LET'S TALK ABOUT IT!

> "Was it easy or hard to know what I was feeling without words?"
>
> "It's always helpful to use our words to tell someone how we're feeling."

CATCH A FEELING

One of the most beloved children's games is playing catch. This exercise will get your child moving while building their emotional and impulse control.

GOOD FOR: Emotional Control, Impulse Control

MATERIALS:

Small- to medium-size ball

TIME NEEDED: 10 minutes

HELPFUL TIP:
If your child seems to quickly lose interest in this activity, try finding a more engaging toy to toss (squishy ball, favorite stuffed animal).

INSTRUCTIONS:

1. Begin the game sitting down on the floor across from your child.
2. Roll the ball to your child and ask them to say a feeling word (happy, sad, mad).
3. Continue rolling the ball back and forth and identifying feelings.
4. After several passes, stand up and continue facing your child.
5. This time, toss the ball to them and have them say, "I feel ________ when ________." They can give a general example or a personal experience.
6. Continue the back-and-forth toss for several more rounds.

LET'S TALK ABOUT IT!

> "I am so proud of how you were using feeling words during the game!"
>
> "Do you remember what a feeling word is?"
>
> "Let's keep practicing using feeling words to describe how we're feeling."

FEEL THE MUSIC

Music is good for the soul and a great way to connect to our emotions. In this game, your child will learn how to not only hear the music but to feel it as well.

GOOD FOR: Emotional Control, Impulse Control

MATERIALS:

4 or 5 different tempos of music (slow, fast)
Phone or something to play music

TIME NEEDED:
10 minutes

HELPFUL TIP:
If your child doesn't prefer to dance, they could simply do the facial expression or draw a picture of the feeling they are thinking of as they listen.

INSTRUCTIONS:

1. To begin the game, explain to your child that we move depending on our emotions.
2. Tell your child that you will play some music and ask them to dance according to how they feel.
3. Allow the music and dancing to continue for 2 or 3 minutes.
4. Switch the music to a different style/genre/beat. Again, ask them to dance how they feel.
5. Continue with the game, inviting your child to choose their own song to dance to.

LET'S TALK ABOUT IT!

"During this game, we danced to several different songs and experienced several different feelings."

"What did you notice about how the music made you feel?"

SOOTHING SENSATIONS

Part of having emotional control means having the ability to stop and be mindful in the moment. In this self-soothing activity, your child will learn a technique known as "grounding," which is an effective coping strategy for uncomfortable feelings.

GOOD FOR: Impulse Control, Emotional Regulation

MATERIALS:

None

TIME NEEDED:
5 minutes

HELPFUL TIP:
Turn this exercise into a game of "I spy" by beginning each prompt with "I spy five things I can see . . ." See if they can guess what your senses are picking up.

LET'S TALK ABOUT IT!

"What big feelings do you think this exercise could help us with?"

INSTRUCTIONS:

1. Begin by finding a quiet spot to sit with your child. Use comfortable seating, such as a cushion on the floor or on the bed.
2. Have your child find a comfortable position, whether sitting or lying down.
3. Begin by telling them that you're going to teach them a soothing activity.
4. Ask them to try and relax their body completely. Take a few big breaths together.
5. Slowly guide them through finding and saying out loud:
   a) 5 things they can see
   b) 4 things they can touch
   c) 3 things they can hear
   d) 2 things they can smell
   e) 1 thing they can taste (or tasted most recently)
6. Check in with how they are feeling.

THE COPING SKILL GAME

An important part of emotional control means knowing healthy ways to calm down. In this game, your child will explore meaningful coping strategies to use for uncomfortable emotions.

GOOD FOR: Emotional Control, Working Memory

MATERIALS:

Dice
Paper
Pencil

TIME NEEDED:
10 minutes

HELPFUL TIP:
Your child may not have many ideas for calming strategies so you may need to help them think of some ideas (deep breathing, counting to 10, drawing their emotion, or asking for a hug).

INSTRUCTIONS:

1. Begin the game by asking your child to name things that make them feel better when they are sad, mad, scared, and so on. Say, "These are called coping skills."
2. Help your child choose an uncomfortable emotion.
3. Give your child the dice and let them roll a number.
4. Whatever number they get is how many coping skills they need to identify for the chosen emotion. (If they pick "mad" and roll a 3, they should say 3 coping skills for anger.)
5. Continue the game by choosing a new feeling, rolling the dice, and exploring healthy strategies for responding to that emotion.

LET'S TALK ABOUT IT!

> "What coping skill would you like to start practicing this week?"

HEAD-TO-TOE EMOTIONS

One of the ways that we experience emotions is through our body sensations. In this activity, your child will improve their emotional awareness by locating where they commonly feel emotions in their body.

GOOD FOR: Emotional Control

MATERIALS:

Paper
Pencil
Crayons

TIME NEEDED:
10 minutes

HELPFUL TIP:
Your child may need extra help understanding body sensations. Use examples such as butterflies in the stomach, goose bumps on the skin, and racing heart.

INSTRUCTIONS:

1. Begin by having your child draw the outline of their body on their paper.
2. To the side of the drawing, have them make a list of emotions they often experience.
3. Now have them pick a color for each feeling and draw a colored dot next to the emotion.
4. Explain to your child that we often experience emotions in different places in our body.
5. Using the coordinating color for each feeling, have them place a dot in the areas of the body they often feel that particular emotion (nervous: head, stomach).
6. Explain to them that these were body sensations that they were experiencing.

LET'S TALK ABOUT IT!

> "Can you tell me about a time when you've experienced an emotion with a body sensation?"

FEELINGS SCAVENGER HUNT

It's common for children to form emotional attachments to objects within their home. In this version of the classic game, your child will go on an emotional scavenger hunt, seeking items that remind them of different feelings.

GOOD FOR: Emotional Control, Working Memory, Flexibility

MATERIALS:

Objects around the house

TIME NEEDED:
15 minutes

HELPFUL TIP:
This would be a great game for siblings to do together to compare and contrast their perceptions and experiences. If your child prefers to be creative, you could invite them to draw their observations.

INSTRUCTIONS:

1. Write a list of feeling words with the help of your child.
2. Give your child the list and instruct them to find one item in the home that reminds them of that feeling.
3. Next to each emotion, have them write down what the object is or bring it to show you.
4. Take a few minutes to explore some of their thoughts and memories related to the objects.

LET'S TALK ABOUT IT!

"What is your favorite item?"

"What is your least favorite item and why?"

READY TO RESPOND?

It's important that your child be able to pause and think before responding with emotion. In this activity, your child will have the opportunity to practice this strategy while thinking through a few scenarios.

GOOD FOR: Emotional Control, Impulse Control, Working Memory

MATERIALS:

Paper
Pencil
Scissors
Red Crayon
Green Crayon

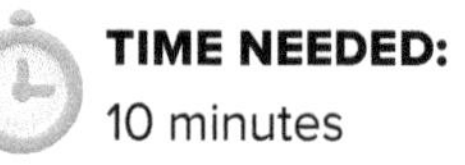

TIME NEEDED:
10 minutes

HELPFUL TIP:
A healthy response to an uncomfortable situation can include taking a time-out or walking away. This activity is a great opportunity to help your child understand that it's okay to walk away or need a moment to cool down before they proceed.

INSTRUCTIONS:

1. First, you'll need to create your scenario cards. Think of a few age-appropriate situations where a child may experience anger, sadness, or any other uncomfortable feeling (losing a board game, being teased, or struggling with math homework).
2. Write a few different situations down and cut them out separately.
3. On the back of each card, describe how the child is thinking, feeling, and acting. (You think about playing again, feel challenged, and say "good game, let's play again" to the other player(s); you think it's unfair and feel embarrassed and angry, so you want to say something mean back to the bully; you feel overwhelmed and think it's too hard, so you want to tear the math assignment in half.)

4. Have your child create two "buzzers," one that is red and one that is green. They will press the green buzzer to answer, "Ready to respond" or the red buzzer to answer "Needs to take a pause."
5. Now it's time to play. Read a scenario to your child and then offer the details on the back.
6. Ask, "Are you ready to respond or do you need to take a pause?"
7. Continue with the same steps as you read through each situation.

LET'S TALK ABOUT IT!

> "Have you ever been in a situation where you needed to pause and think about it?"
> "Why is it important to take that pause sometimes?"

ON THE PAGE ACTIVITY

FEELINGS FORECAST

Much like the weather, our feelings aren't always predictable. This exercise can help your child improve their emotional awareness and be better prepared for future "storms." Read the prompts together, then let your child write or draw additional feelings in the space provided.

WARM AND SUNNY:

A warm and sunny feeling often creates a(n) [circle one: comfortable, uncomfortable] response in the body, such as relaxed muscles, pleasant thoughts, and natural breathing.

My warm and sunny feelings:

____

____

____

CLOUDY AND GRAY:

A cloudy and gray feeling often creates a(n) [circle one: comfortable, uncomfortable] response in the body such as low energy, tearfulness, and stomach/ headaches.

My cloudy and gray feelings:

____

____

____

STORMY AND RAINY:

A stormy and rainy feeling often creates a(n) [circle one: comfortable, uncomfortable] response in the body such as muscle tension, racing heart, and unhelpful thoughts.

My stormy and rainy feelings:

HELPFUL TIP: For younger children, draw a picture of each type of weather and have them point to it as you say different feelings.

LET'S TALK ABOUT IT!

> "What is your emotional forecast for today?"

EMOTIONS PIZZA

In this creative activity, your child will use their growing vocabulary of feeling words to explore their own emotional experiences as they create their "emotions pizza"!

GOOD FOR: Emotional Control, Working Memory

MATERIALS:

Paper
Pencil
Crayons
Scissors and glue (optional)

TIME NEEDED:
15 minutes

HELPFUL TIP:
Sometimes children avoid discussing their uncomfortable feelings. You can remind them that having emotions is what makes us human and it's normal to experience them—even the big, uncomfortable ones.

INSTRUCTIONS:

1. Begin the activity by having your child identify and list five or more feelings they commonly experience. Set aside.
2. Have your child draw a big circle on their paper and explain that they will be creating an "emotions pizza."
3. Invite them to add details, such as the crust, sauce, and cheese, with their crayons.
4. Return to their feelings list and tell them to write down a pizza topping for each emotion (pepperoni = happy, sausage = sad).
5. Lead a conversation about which feelings they feel the most versus which they feel the least.
6. Tell your child to add their toppings of emotions to their pizza! (They may choose to draw them directly on the pizza, or draw, cut, and glue them to it.)

LET'S TALK ABOUT IT!

> "Are there any of these feelings that you would like to feel less often or be able to respond to differently?"

FEELINGS THERMOMETER

Often as children become aware of their feelings, they struggle to know when to ask for help. In this activity, your child will relate emotional intensity to their body temperature as they continue improving their emotional control.

GOOD FOR: Emotional Control

MATERIALS:

Paper
Pencil
Crayons
Analog thermometer for visual reference (optional)

TIME NEEDED:
10 minutes

INSTRUCTIONS:

1. Begin by discussing a time when your child took medicine for a fever. Remind them that their body needed a little help cooling off.
2. Help your child draw a large thermometer on their paper.
3. Add the numbers 1 through 5 to the thermometer, starting with the 5 at the top. Separate the levels with lines.
4. Starting from the bottom, work with your child on adding feeling words to the appropriate number. Provide them with examples, such as "A level 1 feeling may include calm, happy, safe, content, relaxed. A level 5 may include terrified or furious."
5. Continue until each level has at least one feeling word.
6. Have your child choose a color for each level and color in each section.

HELPFUL TIP:
As your child is thinking about their levels of emotion, prompt them to use their body sensations to help them identify their feelings (muscles are tense, hard to breathe, fast heartbeat stomach/head hurts). You could ask, "What sensations in your body help you know that this is a level 3 feeling?" Once complete, consider hanging this picture somewhere in your home where your child can see.

7. Engage your child in a conversation about their levels of emotion. Discuss what feels comfortable, small, and manageable, and big and overwhelming.

8. Identify the level(s) where your child needs to seek an adult's help. Draw a large red square around that area.

LET'S TALK ABOUT IT!

"What is something you could do on your own if you're at a level 3?"

"What is something you could do with an adult's help if you're at a level 5?"

Key Takeaways

Although it can be challenging, staying in control of our emotions is an important skill to support healthy relationships. Being open about your mistakes will teach your child that it's okay to mess up and help them set realistic expectations for themselves. With the proper example, children can learn how to acknowledge their feelings and choose healthy ways to cope in times of discomfort.

- The challenge with emotions is not that we feel them but how we choose to manage them.
- The truth is that children are still learning how to control their emotions and are looking to their parents for inspiration.
- When emotional control is consistently practiced in the home, your child will pick up on those healthy habits.
- One of the greatest gifts you can offer your child is the gift of an emotionally healthy parent.

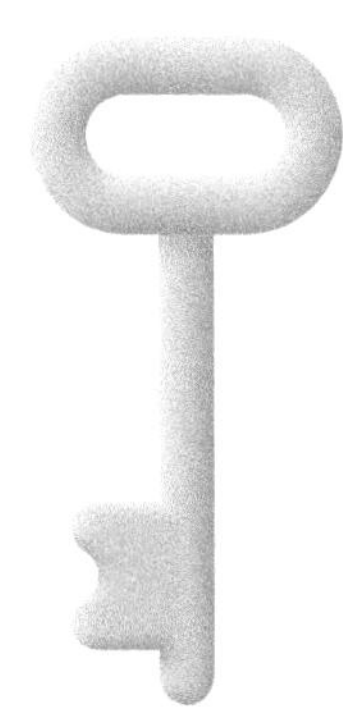

CHAPTER 6

Improve Your Attention Span

We live in an extremely noisy world that is constantly stimulating our senses. As adults, we recognize that sometimes we must make an effort to reduce the interruptions. We use strategies such as "Do Not Disturb" on our smartphones, we close doors to limit noise, and at times we ask not to be bothered, all to help ourselves stay focused.

Children tend to be less aware of their own needs and do not always have the option to alter their environment. Instead, they must learn how to adapt their mindset and use what resources they have. That's why we will explore the topic of attention and persistence in this chapter, alongside various strategies for improving focus.

BEHAVIORAL OR SOMETHING ELSE

When I first met eight-year-old Jack, it was evident that he had difficulty staying focused and controlling his body. As we talked, he had difficulty sitting in the chair and struggled to complete a simple thought. His eyes darted around the room, searching for the activity that he wanted to do. I knew in that moment that Jack would benefit from plenty of movement and fun during his treatment. Unfortunately, many adults don't understand that children learn and communicate through play and movement.

Jack had been living with his grandfather, who said he felt confident in meeting Jack's basic needs but was honest in that he struggled to discipline Jack. He described how Jack was often "disrespectful," interrupting conversations and moving "a thousand miles a minute." Jack had already been receiving accommodations at school that were unsuccessful. After further evaluation, Jack was given the diagnosis of ADHD. Despite his progress in therapy, Jack continued to have difficulties at home and school. With his grandfather's approval, Jack was referred for medication management. After several exhausting months of no progress, Jack's grandfather began to report small victories at home, such as Jack staying focused for homework or being able to sit almost entirely through dinner.

Although medicine can be a viable option for some children, psychotropic medication should be considered with caution as it alters the chemical makeup of the brain and nervous system and can have serious side effects. In the case of Jack, it was a combination of therapy strategies and medication that helped him become successful.

Everyday Strategies to Build Attention

Because brains are unique and ever-changing, you must be open and flexible when thinking about attention-building strategies. What helps you focus may not be helpful for me, and vice versa. You need to keep this in mind when thinking about your child. Naturally, we want to offer strategies to our children that we have found to be effective for ourselves. So, when they are resistant or the plan doesn't work, it can appear as a lack of effort. Remember to remain patient and open-minded during this process, as it can take your child much trial and error to find what fits.

Our childhoods inform our parenting, but we must remember that things change. The old idea of whole-body listening, which required a child to be still and make eye contact for effective learning, has been disproven. In fact, your child may learn more from moving more. For example, recent brain research has found that by incorporating play and movement into the classroom, children actually learn more. Pay attention the next time you give your child directions. Are they playing or moving while you talk? How might you have interpreted this before reading this book? No worries! Now you can move forward in setting your child up for the most success.

Encourage them to reflect the expectations by asking, "So, what are you supposed to be doing?" to ensure they understand. Another approach is to create a "focus toolbox." Be sure to use the term "tool" instead of "toy." Simply store a variety of fidgets, either store-bought or homemade (A Fidget for Focus, page 101), in an open container somewhere that is easily accessible to your child. Finally, keep in mind that it's extremely hard to concentrate with a tired brain or empty stomach. When in doubt, offer a snack or moment to relax before starting any structured tasks.

MINDFUL MUSICIAN

Get ready to make some music! In this activity, your child will keep the beat while they work on maintaining their attention.

GOOD FOR: Sustained Attention and Goal-Oriented Persistence, Impulse Control

MATERIALS:

Plastic container with lid (water bottle, bowl, etc.)
Uncooked pasta, rice, or beans

TIME NEEDED:
15 minutes

HELPFUL TIP:

For a fun challenge, try singing a song to the rhythm of the beat.

If your child loses focus, teach them to mindfully reset with a deep breath, then start again.

INSTRUCTIONS:

1. Work with your child on creating your own musical instruments by pouring some of the dried foods into the container. Tightly secure the lid.
2. Create multiple instruments and invite family members and friends to join the music circle. Consider using different ingredients to create lots of sounds.
3. Invite your child to mindfully listen to each sound and choose their favorite.
4. Have your child create a beat with their instrument as you follow along.
5. Take turns leading the rhythm until everyone has had a turn.

LET'S TALK ABOUT IT!

"Did you know that music can actually help us focus and get things done?"

Explore with your child ways they could use music to help them complete a task like singing the cleanup song while picking up toys or listening to instrumental music while practicing reading.

COUNT THE BUBBLES

This game is bubbles of fun! In this exercise, your child will practice holding their attention and improve their counting skills.

GOOD FOR: Sustained Attention and Goal-Oriented Persistence, Impulse Control

MATERIALS:

Bottle of bubbles

TIME NEEDED:
5 minutes

HELPFUL TIP:
Your child may be tempted to pop the bubbles. Consider allowing them to freely play with the bubbles for a few minutes before starting the game.

INSTRUCTIONS:

1. First, invite your child outside for some outdoor playtime. Bring the bubbles!
2. Begin blowing the bubbles and ask your child to count how many they see.
3. Next, give them a few different challenges to do while they're counting (spin and count, jump on one leg and count).
4. Tell them they must count all the bubbles before they pop!
5. Continue blowing the bubbles and having your child quickly count them.

LET'S TALK ABOUT IT!

If your child was counting out loud for this exercise, try saying, "I noticed that you were counting out loud during the game. Was that helpful for you to focus?" If they were not counting aloud, explore what strategies they feel were effective for them during the game.

NOW YOU SEE IT

In this tricky game, your child will exercise their focus as they try to figure out a magic act.

GOOD FOR: Sustained Attention and Goal-Oriented Persistence

MATERIALS:

Small object
2 matching cups

TIME NEEDED:
10 minutes

HELPFUL TIP:
Add a third cup to the mix for an added challenge!

INSTRUCTIONS:

1. Begin by showing your child the object and allowing them to watch you place it under one of the cups.
2. Tell your child to stay focused on that cup.
3. With both cups upside down on the table, slowly begin sliding them and rearranging their position. Repeat several times.
4. Have your child guess which cup has the object underneath.
5. Switch places, allowing your child to hide the object this time.
6. Continue until someone correctly guesses the cup with the object.

LET'S TALK ABOUT IT!

"Did your mind ever get tired of following the cup?" Discuss how it's normal for our brains to get tired and lose focus, especially if there's a lot going on (such as several moving cups).

PASTA CREATIONS

Threading objects on a string is a task that requires a significant amount of focus and determination. This activity will allow your child the opportunity to get creative while improving their executive skills.

GOOD FOR: Sustained Attention and Goal-Oriented Persistence, Impulse Control

MATERIALS:

String (any kind will do)
Scissors
Beads, dried pasta, buttons, foam shapes, etc.

TIME NEEDED:
15 minutes

HELPFUL TIP:

If your child enjoys jewelry-making and already has their own kit, invite them to pull it out and use it for this exercise!

Depending on your materials, this activity may prove to be quite difficult for your child and they may require some help. Be sure to wait until they ask—and be ready and willing to assist.

INSTRUCTIONS:

1. Begin by setting up the materials on a table. Consider placing the objects in separate bowls so they are easily accessible.
2. Help your child cut their string to the length they prefer.
3. Instruct your child to create their own jewelry, key chain, or craft using the materials.

LET'S TALK ABOUT IT!

"I'm proud of you for asking me for help."

"Sometimes when things get too hard, we need to ask an adult for help."

"What can happen if we decide *not* to ask for help?"

COLOR AND CONCENTRATE

In this color-by-numbers exercise, your child will need to use attention to detail to color a picture according to your directions.

GOOD FOR: Sustained Attention and Goal-Oriented Persistence, Working Memory

MATERIALS:

Paper
Pencil
Crayons

TIME NEEDED:
15 minutes

HELPFUL TIP:
Consider helping your child develop a strategy to keep them on task, such as coloring all the 5s first, then 4s, and so on.

INSTRUCTIONS:

1. Prepare this activity by first drawing a large picture with various details. Divide the picture into small sections.
2. Somewhere on the paper, identify the colors to be used in the picture and give each color a number (1 = green, 2 = blue).
3. Begin labeling the pieces of the picture with the number of the coordinating colors.
4. Give your child the picture and instruct them to color it according to the numbers.

LET'S TALK ABOUT IT!

> "In this activity, it was important for you to pay close attention to the numbers. What would have happened if you lost focus and miscolored an area?"

ALPHABET SOUP

In this activity, your child will use their ability to stay focused as they look for letters in their soup!

GOOD FOR: Sustained Attention and Goal-Oriented Persistence

MATERIALS:

Set of all 26 letters (toy set, bath set, or handmade using paper, pencil, and scissors)
Bowl
Large spoon
Food item with pasta letters (optional)

TIME NEEDED:
10 minutes

HELPFUL TIP:
To increase the challenge, have your child name something that starts with each letter or have them find each letter in their name. If your child gets stuck on finding a letter, teach them how to skip it and come back.

INSTRUCTIONS:

1. Begin by gathering the alphabet. If you don't have a set, make your own by writing each letter on paper and cutting them out individually. Ensure that all 26 letters are present.
2. If you are using a food item, prepare it as instructed.
3. Add the letters or prepared food into a bowl and mix them up well.
4. Have your child sit down with the bowl and a spoon and try to find each letter, starting with A.
5. Each time they find a letter, have them separate it from the rest (on the side of the bowl or on the table).
6. Continue until they find all 26 letters!

LET'S TALK ABOUT IT!

"Great job on finding your letters!"

"Do you think it was helpful to skip some of the letters that you couldn't find?"

THE CLEANUP GAME

In this activity, a commonly dreaded task will be turned into a game to help your child practice maintaining focus and staying oriented to their goal.

GOOD FOR: Sustained Attention and Goal-Oriented Persistence, Working Memory

MATERIALS:

Room with various toys/items (bedroom or playroom)

TIME NEEDED:
10 minutes

HELPFUL TIP:
Depending on your child's development, you may need to offer more or less support to them during the game. For extra silly fun, make special rules such as using oven mitts on hands.

INSTRUCTIONS:

1. Have the game take place in a room that needs tidying.
2. Tell your child you are challenging them to a race and assign the items they will pick up. Let them know what items you will be in charge of.
3. Set usual expectations for cleaning up (toys must go in their rightful place).
4. Say "On your mark, get set, go!"
5. Race your child to get all the items picked up.
6. Whoever puts away all of their items first wins! Make sure to have a great prize for the winner.

LET'S TALK ABOUT IT!

> "Sometimes a challenge can help us stay focused."
> "What other tasks could we turn into a game?"

COUNT ME IN

In this math memory game, your child will need to practice concentrating to remember the number of coins they observe.

GOOD FOR: Sustained Attention and Goal-Oriented Persistence, Working Memory

MATERIALS:

Coins
Small cloth

TIME NEEDED:
10 minutes

HELPFUL TIP:
Teach your child to say what they see to help their brain focus and remember.

INSTRUCTIONS:

1. Let your child know that you are going to challenge their memory and focus.
2. Lay several coins in front of them (take note of how many there are).
3. Give your child a few seconds to study them, then quickly cover them with the cloth!
4. Once they are out of sight, tell your child if they can correctly identify the amount of coins there were, they will get to keep them all!
5. Continue the game by changing the number of coins and limiting the time your child can observe them.

LET'S TALK ABOUT IT!

"Was it harder to concentrate on the coins knowing that they would soon be out of sight?" Discuss how it's important to take visual and written notes to help our brain focus on the details.

IT ALL ADDS UP

Here's another math game your child will surely love. In this fun game, your child will need to practice focusing as they count money.

GOOD FOR: Sustained Attention and Goal-Oriented Persistence, Working Memory

MATERIALS:

Paper
Pencil
Money (real or pretend)

TIME NEEDED:
10 minutes

HELPFUL TIP:
If you find that counting money is beyond your child's developmental level, try playing "store" and simply having them sort the money by dollars and coins.

INSTRUCTIONS:

1. Using the paper, write down (or draw) three items that your child would usually like to purchase.
2. Give each item a reasonable price.
3. Hand your child the money and ask which item they would like to buy first.
4. Help your child count out the exact change to give to you.
5. Continue with the game until they have "bought" all the items.

LET'S TALK ABOUT IT!

> "I had fun playing this game with you! Counting [or sorting] money takes a lot of concentration. What could help us stay focused when we're doing this task?"

DON'T LET IT DROP

Keeping an object in motion requires focus and determination. In this activity, your child will practice focusing their attention on one thing as they maintain a goal.

GOOD FOR: Sustained Attention and Goal-Oriented Persistence, Impulse Control

MATERIALS:

Balloon (or ball)

TIME NEEDED:
15 minutes

HELPFUL TIP:
For an added challenge, try taking a step back each time the object touches the ground. If using a balloon, consider using a stick to keep it afloat.

INSTRUCTIONS:

1. Blow up the balloon (or grab a soft ball).
2. Move to an open space in your home or take the game outside.
3. Instruct your child to keep the object in the air and don't let it drop!
4. Count how many times each person touches the object.

LET'S TALK ABOUT IT!

"Did you notice how you needed to stay focused on the balloon (ball) to keep it going?"

Talk about how we use focus for many things, from schoolwork to games!

ON THE PAGE ACTIVITY

FOCUS FOR FUN

In this exercise, your child will practice paying close attention as they answer some fun questions about themselves. Read these questions to your child and record their answers.

1. Something I love to do for fun is ______________________.
2. My favorite color is ______________________.
3. Something I dislike doing is ______________________.
4. I once ______________________ and I felt really proud!
5. My favorite food is ______________________.
6. My best friend's name is ______________________.
7. If I could go anywhere in the world, I would visit ______________________.
8. ______________________ is something that makes me angry.
9. I want to ______________________ when I grow up.
10. Three things that I love about myself are:

    ______________________,

    ______________________,

    ______________________.

HELPFUL TIP: This is a great opportunity to bond with your child! Don't worry, they'll get to ask you questions in the next chapter.

LET'S TALK ABOUT IT!

"I enjoyed getting to hear your answers!"

"Some of these questions were similar but different. Have you come across this at school before?"

"How can you avoid misreading a question?"

A FIDGET FOR FOCUS

The tiny tools meant to improve focus known as "fidgets" are loved by children everywhere. For this activity, your child will get to create their own fidget to add to their collection.

GOOD FOR: Task Initiation, Sustained Attention and Goal-Oriented Persistence, Impulse Control

MATERIALS:

Empty, dry water bottle
Funnel or a piece of paper
½ cup of flour (or cornstarch, baking soda, sand, or water beads)
Pack of balloons (or just one that you have lying around)

TIME NEEDED:
15 minutes

HELPFUL TIP:
Be sure to teach your child how to use their new stress ball. Show them how hard they can squeeze and set ground rules for proper use, if needed.

INSTRUCTIONS:

1. First, ensure that you have all the materials prepared on the table.
2. Let your child know that you will be helping them create their very own fidget in the form of a stress ball.
3. Have them hold the bottle while you use the funnel to pour the flour inside. If you don't have a funnel, pour the ingredients onto a piece of paper. Loosely fold the paper and use it to guide the ingredients into the bottle.
4. Once completed, carefully secure a balloon over the top.
5. Instruct your child to slowly flip the bottle upside down to allow the flour to slide into the balloon.
6. With the flour inside the balloon, carefully remove the balloon from the bottle and tie a knot.
7. That's it! Your new fidget tool and stress reliever is ready to help!

LET'S TALK ABOUT IT!

"Does using this feel good? What do you like about it?" Discuss scenarios where the tool would best be used.

RELAX AND FOCUS

Mindfulness is a practice that can benefit us in a variety of ways. In this exercise, your child will work on being mindfully aware of their attention as you gently guide them through a meditation.

GOOD FOR: Sustained Attention and Goal-Oriented Persistence, Emotional Control, Impulse Control

MATERIALS:

None

TIME NEEDED:
10 minutes

HELPFUL TIP:
It may be challenging for your child to mindfully concentrate on an imaginary scene in their mind. Remember that these skills become easier with practice. Consider using a favorite memory as the imaginary scene to use for next time.

LET'S TALK ABOUT IT!

"Did you sometimes feel like your thoughts were hard to control during this exercise? This is normal! The more we practice this skill, the easier it will get."

INSTRUCTIONS:

1. Find a relaxing spot for this activity.
2. Invite your child to find a comfortable position (whether seated or lying down).
3. Tell your child they can close their eyes or lower the gaze to the floor.
4. Begin by having your child breathe in through their nose for 4 seconds, then out through their mouth for 4 seconds. Practice this a few times.
5. Guide your child through a relaxing story, such as a sailboat that is casually floating on the water.
6. Engage their senses by having them notice the sights, sounds, smells, and other sensations in the story.
7. Remind them to continue those relaxing belly breaths throughout this exercise.
8. Continue describing the imaginary for 5 minutes or as long as your child is willing.
9. When they're ready, help them bring their awareness back to the present by describing the sights and smells within the room as they open their eyes.

Key Takeaways

Your child's brain is still developing, so they rely on you to provide temporary support while they strengthen their skills. Help them explore strategic ways to keep themselves focused and on task, such as reading aloud or listening to music. Instinctively, children may need to move their body to be at their cognitive best. Check in to see if they are listening and be prepared to offer a gentle prompt to get them back on course.

- Children tend to be less aware of their own needs and do not always have the option to alter their environment.
- They must learn how to adapt their mindset and use what resources they have.
- Remember to remain patient and open-minded during this process, as it can take your child many trial-and-error attempts to find what fits.
- When in doubt, offer a snack or moment to relax before starting any structured tasks.

CHAPTER 7

Learn How to Start Tasks

Many adults and children alike struggle with task initiation. Sometimes it's hard to pause an enjoyable activity or begin on a big project or task that feels overwhelming. Whatever the reason, getting started can be a challenge for anyone. In this chapter, your child will learn what it takes to initiate tasks on their own while exploring inventive and creative ways to have fun.

UNMOTIVATED AND UNHAPPY

Josie's parents came to me when she was ten years old with one primary concern—she was "extremely anxious about everything." During the intake session, her mom disclosed that Josie came from a long line of people with mental health struggles. She described various family members who had anxiety disorders, ADHD, and depression. Her mom became tearful as she described her own challenges with anxiety and depression, admitting that Josie had observed her have a few breakdowns. She was deeply worried about how this may have affected her daughter.

Josie was indeed struggling with severe anxiety that was hindering her ability to be successful. During sessions, Josie would often wait for approval before moving out of her chair and was severely uncomfortable with activities that required ingenuity. As her confidence level declined, so did her amount of success. Josie was locked into a vicious cycle of anxiety and learned helplessness. After many months of cognitive behavioral therapy (CBT) with elements of art and play, Josie evolved into a different kid. She found healthier ways to manage her stress and learned how to recognize the inaccurate thoughts that were often the barrier to her intrinsic motivation. Josie's mom and dad participated in several parenting sessions and were able to learn effective strategies to help support Josie outside of therapy. In using her strategies, Josie was able to feel more motivated, encouraged, and self-confident.

Everyday Strategies to Build Task Initiation

From the moment that we wake up, our prefrontal cortex is propelling us forward to get things done. Knowing that this part of a child's brain is "under construction" can help us understand why they often struggle with self-motivation. It's not that they don't want to do it without you, it's that they lack the ability. For children, putting their mind and body into action takes meaningful effort that can be difficult for them to do alone. The space between thought and action for them can seem vast so they quickly lose interest. The problem is parents often misinterpret this behavior as a deliberate act of defiance.

If you find yourself having to administer consequences frequently, this could be a sign that your expectations are too high. Ask yourself, "What is my child truly capable of and how do I know?" On a similar note, be sure that your child isn't relying on you too much. Children need plenty of opportunities to flex their independence muscle. By giving your child age-appropriate responsibilities at home, this will give them a supportive space to explore their capabilities and practice using intrinsic motivation to achieve success.

PICTURE THIS

In this classic guessing game, your child will practice task initiation by choosing an idea and drawing a picture for you to guess.

GOOD FOR: Task Initiation

MATERIALS:

Paper
Pencil

TIME NEEDED:
10 minutes

HELPFUL TIP:
Remember that the goal of this exercise is to help your child with thinking on their own, so try to allow them the independence to form their own unique ideas.

INSTRUCTIONS:

1. Explain to your child that you're going to play a game of Guess the Picture.
2. Tell your child to think of something to draw, then begin drawing it on the paper.
3. As they draw, you can ask questions about the picture and try to guess what it is.
4. Once you've finished, switch roles and see who can figure out the drawing in the least amount of time.

LET'S TALK ABOUT IT!

"Was it hard to think of what to draw?"
"How did you decide?"

FULL OF THOUGHT

Another great way to improve self-initiative is through altruism. In this activity, your child will exercise their task initiation skills by creating a handmade card for someone.

GOOD FOR: Task Initiation, Sustained Attention and Goal-Oriented Persistence

MATERIALS:

Paper
Pencil
Crayons
Glue, scissors, art supplies (optional)

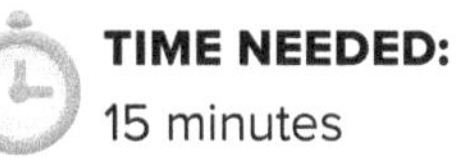

TIME NEEDED:
15 minutes

HELPFUL TIP:
Remember that this exercise is to strengthen their task initiation skills, so try not to help unless they ask.

INSTRUCTIONS:

1. Let your child know that they will be creating a homemade card (get well, birthday, thank you) for someone. This could be someone they know or a complete stranger.
2. Sit with them and ask them to share their inspiration as they color. You could ask, "What do you like about this person?" or "Tell me about a time they made you smile."
3. Once completed, create a plan to deliver the card to the designated person.

LET'S TALK ABOUT IT!

"How do you think this card will make ____________ feel?" Discuss the importance of altruism and doing kind things for other people.

HIDE-AND-SEEK WITH STUFFIES

This is an activity your child is sure to love! In this version of hide-and-seek, your child will use original thinking and self-motivation to choose where to hide their favorite stuffed toy for you to find.

GOOD FOR: Task Initiation

MATERIALS:

Stuffed toy

TIME NEEDED:
10 minutes

HELPFUL TIP:
To increase the challenge, have your child hide several toys in various places for you to find.

INSTRUCTIONS:

1. First, have your child pick a stuffed toy to use for the game.
2. Instruct your child that while you close your eyes and count to 10, they will go hide their toy somewhere in the house.
3. When you finish counting, say, "Ready or not, here I come!"
4. Search for the toy until you find it.
5. Switch roles if your child is interested.

LET'S TALK ABOUT IT!

"You picked some great hiding spots!" Praise and discuss your child's ability to think on their own.

BUILDING IDEAS

A surefire way to get your child's ideas flowing is through building with blocks. In this activity, your child will exercise their task initiation skills through creating a structure with plastic bricks. It may appear basic, but this activity is about practicing authentic play with your child.

GOOD FOR: Task Initiation, Impulse Control

MATERIALS:

Plastic building bricks (or any kind of blocks)

TIME NEEDED: 15 minutes

HELPFUL TIP:
If your child needs a little inspiration, try giving them a vague category such as "a building in the city" or something from their favorite story.

INSTRUCTIONS:

1. Sit down with your child with a box of plastic building bricks or blocks and enthusiastically say, "'I'm excited to build something with you!"
2. Ask if they would like you to help them build theirs or build your own.
3. As you're building, try saying what you observe. ("I see you're adding a structure to the side" or "I notice you're separating the colors.")
4. Praise their ideas by saying something like "I love the way you're stacking them large to small."
5. Enjoy this quality playtime with your child.

LET'S TALK ABOUT IT!

"Sometimes it's hard to know where to begin."

Encourage your child to ask for help when they find a task confusing or too difficult.

ULTIMATE FREEZE DANCE

It's back! In this rendition of the classic freeze game, your child will use their own ideas to add some originality to the game.

GOOD FOR: Task Initiation, Working Memory, Impulse Control

MATERIALS:

Music that can be paused
Phone or something to play music on

TIME NEEDED:
15 minutes

HELPFUL TIP:
For added fun, allow your child to choose the music for the game!

INSTRUCTIONS:

1. Before you begin, explain to your child that you want to play another round of the freeze dance game.
2. Explain that each time the music starts, they will choose a new rule for everyone to follow (hop like a bunny, slither like a snake, twirl like a leaf).
3. Continue the game and switch roles if they'd like.

LET'S TALK ABOUT IT!

"It can be a big responsibility to create your own rules."
"Was this a difficult or easy task for you?"

WHATEVER YOU SAY

Being in charge requires a strong sense of self-motivation, and what kid doesn't want to be the boss? In this game of follow the leader, your child will initiate movements for you to follow!

GOOD FOR: Task Initiation, Emotional Control, Impulse Control

MATERIALS:

None

TIME NEEDED:
15 minutes

HELPFUL TIP:
Invite the family to join in on the game! Your child will likely enjoy the attention and leadership.

INSTRUCTIONS:

1. Introduce the game by saying, "Let's play a game of follow the leader!"
2. Stand or sit face-to-face.
3. Tell your child that they are in charge. You will mirror whatever they do.
4. As they move or talk, you copy them.
5. Now switch roles and have them copy you.

LET'S TALK ABOUT IT!

"How did it feel to have someone copying your every move?"

"It was fun and silly to copy each other for a little while, but it's important that we can be ourselves once the game is over." Discuss how important our own thoughts and ideas are.

IT'S ALL AN ACT

Invite the family and neighborhood friends over for a fun game night! In this classic game of charades, your child will use several executive skills including task initiation to act out various scenes.

GOOD FOR: Task Initiation, Impulse Control, Emotional Control, Flexibility

MATERIALS:

Paper
Pencil
Timer

TIME NEEDED:
15 minutes

HELPFUL TIP:
Although fun with a group, this game is just as fun and effective with you and your child. Take turns trying to guess the scene before the timer runs out. See who can reach five correct guesses first!

INSTRUCTIONS:

1. Start by asking your child to help set up the game.
2. Write down scenarios on square pieces of paper and cut them out.
3. Write the category on the back (emotions, children's movies, activities).
4. Make several scenarios (climbing a tree, feeling sad, playing tag) for each category and organize them together.
5. Stack the cards with the category facing up.
6. To begin, each person will need a partner.
7. The youngest player goes first by choosing a card and acting out what it says.
8. If the partner can guess the scene correctly within one minute, their team gets two points.
9. Ten points wins the game!

LET'S TALK ABOUT IT!

> "In this game, the cards gave us the idea, then we were able to bring the idea to life."
>
> "It's important that you know you're allowed to ask for help anytime you need it." Discuss the importance of asking for help.

COLORS OF THREE

As simple as it seems, coloring is an art form that requires self-motivation. In this activity, your child will use coloring to practice putting their ideas into action.

GOOD FOR: Task Initiation, Flexibility

MATERIALS:

Crayons
Paper

TIME NEEDED:
10 minutes

HELPFUL TIP:
For this activity, consider sitting with your child and encouraging imaginative thinking. Ask your child, "What do these colors make you think of?"

INSTRUCTIONS:

1. Start by setting out the crayons and a piece of paper.
2. Instruct your child to close their eyes and pick three colors.
3. Once they have chosen the colors, tell them they must draw a picture with those colors only.
4. Once complete, invite your child to choose 3 colors for you to draw with.
5. Invite your child to offer their ideas for your drawing.
6. Compare your pictures at the end. Embrace the uniqueness and creativity of their ideas.

LET'S TALK ABOUT IT!

"How did you know where to start with your picture?" Discuss with your child that to create a new idea, we need to know where to begin.

THIS 'N' THAT

Children often have a natural love for being in the kitchen. In this activity, your child will awaken their inner chef as they combine ingenuity, science, and ingredients to create their own recipe.

GOOD FOR: Task Initiation, Impulse Control, Flexibility, Sustained Attention and Goal-Oriented Persistence

MATERIALS:

Bowl
Spoon
Various ingredients of their choosing

INGREDIENT IDEAS:

Honey
Powdered sugar
Fruit
Cereal
Peanut butter
Cocoa powder
Graham crackers
Food coloring

TIME NEEDED:
15 minutes

HELPFUL TIP:

Use active listening ("You're thinking about adding sugar for sweetness") and keep in mind, messes can be cleaned!

INSTRUCTIONS:

1. Set out a bowl and a spoon.
2. Depending on your child's development, you may choose to preselect the ingredients you would feel comfortable with your child using.
3. Introduce your child to the activity by explaining that you're giving them the freedom to create their own recipe.
4. Instruct them to think carefully about each ingredient and consider which ingredients would go well together.
5. If the food items are not preselected, explain that they will need to explore the kitchen and find the ingredients they need.
6. Stay close by and allow your child the space to explore their ideas.
7. Invite them to share their recipe with you!

LET'S TALK ABOUT IT!

"I really enjoyed watching your creativity at work!"

"Did you have a recipe in mind, or did you figure it out along the way?"

RIDDLE ME THIS

In this exercise, your child will be challenged to create a riddle as they practice initiating something new.

GOOD FOR: Task Initiation, Flexibility, Working Memory

MATERIALS:

Paper
Pencil

TIME NEEDED:
10 minutes

HELPFUL TIP:
Keep in mind that these exercises are meant to be fun! If your child seems uninterested in this activity or any others, feel free to move on to a different one.

INSTRUCTIONS:

1. First, tell your child a riddle or a joke ("What starts with a T, ends with a T, and has T in it? A teapot!")
2. Now tell your child to create their own riddle (or joke, song, or poem).
3. Give your child a piece of paper and a pencil and plenty of time to think.
4. Once they are finished, invite them to share their creation with you and other family members.

LET'S TALK ABOUT IT!

"In order for us to create something new, we need to be inspired by something."

"What inspired your riddle (or joke, song, or poem)?"

A THOUGHTFUL ADVENTURE

When we explore our environment, one of the skills we use is task initiation. In this adventure-filled activity, your child will create their own scavenger hunt as they practice exploring new ideas.

GOOD FOR: Task Initiation, Sustained Attention and Goal-Oriented Persistence

MATERIALS:

Paper
Pencil
Camera (optional)

TIME NEEDED:
15 minutes

HELPFUL TIP:
If your child needs a little inspiration to get started, try helping them identify a theme (plants and flowers, colorful objects, things that are round).

INSTRUCTIONS:

1. Begin by explaining the process of a scavenger hunt.
2. Tell your child they will be creating their own!
3. Have them make a list of items to be searched for (outdoor or indoor).
4. You may give your child some space as they explore their thoughts and ideas.
5. Once the list is completed, invite your child to lead you through their scavenger hunt.
6. If you choose, take pictures of each item just like a real explorer.
7. Enjoy following your child's list and locating each of the items!

LET'S TALK ABOUT IT!

"You really put some thought into this activity, and I had so much fun with you!"

"Did you notice yourself thinking about the other person who would be doing the scavenger hunt?" Talk about extrinsic motivators, such as entertaining someone else.

OVERCOMING OBSTACLES

Here's something that is sure to get your child thinking and moving! In this playful game, your child will use objects from around the house to create their own obstacle course.

GOOD FOR: Task Initiation, Flexibility

MATERIALS:

Timer

SUGGESTED OUTDOOR MATERIALS:

Chalk to create hopscotch
Jump rope for the finish line (or an added jump rope challenge)
Bubbles
Hula-Hoop
Ball

SUGGESTED INDOOR MATERIALS:

Pillows to create a "tumbling wall"
Blankets draped across furniture to create a "low crawl" tunnel
String for the finish line

TIME NEEDED: 15 minutes

INSTRUCTIONS:

1. Begin by discussing with your child the various components of an obstacle course.
2. Let them know that they get to create one of their own.
3. You may choose to give them a list of approved materials they are allowed to use or give them the freedom to choose (with the exception of breakables and safety concerns).
4. Be sure to set the expectation of indoor or outdoor use if necessary.
5. Encourage your child to begin setting the course up as they think of ideas. Offer to help if they need an extra set of hands.
6. Once the obstacle course is complete, be sure to take a moment to admire their work and praise their ideas.

HELPFUL TIP:
This is a game that may require a little guidance depending on your child's capabilities. After giving them time to explore their thoughts, ask your child, "How can I help?" Allow them to guide you from there.

7. Grab the family and enjoy competing for the best time to the finish line!

LET'S TALK ABOUT IT!

"Did you enjoy building the obstacle course as much as you liked going through it?"

"Was it difficult to have to put it back together each time?" Use this opportunity to recognize that we often don't prefer the work, but the outcome is what motivates us!

PARENT INTERVIEW

Since becoming a parent, getting to know your child has been high on your priority list. Just the same, your child wants to get to know you better, too! In this activity, your child will practice task initiation by asking you prompted questions as well as some of their own. For younger children, parents may want to write their answers in or encourage them to draw pictures.

1. Something they love to do for fun is ______________________________.
2. Their favorite color is ______________________________.
3. Something they dislike doing is ______________________________.
4. They once ______________________________ and felt really proud!
5. Their favorite food is ______________________________.
6. Kid's question: ______________________________.

   Parent's answer: ______________________________.
7. Kid's question: ______________________________.

   Parent's answer: ______________________________.

continued

PARENT INTERVIEW continued

8. Kid's question: ______________________________.

Parent's answer: ______________________________.

9. Kid's question: ______________________________.

Parent's answer: ______________________________.

10. Kid's question: ______________________________.

Parent's answer: ______________________________.

HELPFUL TIP: It may be difficult for your child to think of their own questions. Consider taking a break from the activity and coming back to it.

LET'S TALK ABOUT IT!

"Sometimes we need to walk away from a task and come back to it." Explain how taking a break from something can help our brain think more clearly.

Key Takeaways

Being a self-starter is an advanced ability that takes time for kids to develop. To initiate a task on their own, they must first feel confident in their abilities. Consider times when your child seems the most resistant to a direction and offer your support. When we examine the reason behind a child's perceived lack of effort, we find that they are simply needing more help to be successful.

- Many adults and children alike struggle with task initiation.
- From the moment that we wake up, our prefrontal cortex is propelling us forward to get things done.
- Knowing that this part of a child's brain is "under construction" can help us understand why they often struggle with self-motivation.
- It's not that they don't want to do it without you, it's that they lack the ability.
- By empowering your child to think of their own ideas at home, this will give them a supportive space to explore their capabilities and practice using intrinsic motivation to achieve success.

CHAPTER 8

Practice Planning and Prioritizing

Although not every aspect of our lives is predictable, having a generalized idea or plan provides the stability we need as human beings to thrive. When unforeseen circumstances do arise, we can simply modify the plan and keep moving forward. Children need plenty of time and experience to effectively develop these skills. In this chapter, you will find games and activities centered around helping your child learn how to plan and prioritize successfully.

PLANNED SUCCESS

Jace began therapy when he was ten years old. His parents explained that he was struggling with his grades in school and his "laziness and disrespect" was a point of tension at home. Jace's teachers would say that his test grades reflect that he knows the material, but he lacked effort in class. At home, Jace would play his video game constantly and ignore his parents' requests to complete his chores. When confronted, he would reply, "I don't care," which often turned into screaming matches between him and his mom.

During therapy, Jace disclosed that he genuinely wanted to improve but didn't know how. He expressed feeling hopeless, that no matter how hard he tried, his effort was never good enough. After further evaluation, it was found that Jace indeed had ADHD with a combined presentation, which was originally missed due to his lack of hyperactivity.

With simple strategies put into place at home and school, Jace began to find a rhythm that enabled him to better plan and prioritize his daily tasks. At home, his parents began using various visual schedules such as a large family calendar, chore charts, and to-do lists. At school, Jace used checklists and highlighters to complete tasks on time while his teachers offered additional check-ins to help him stay on schedule. It goes to show that children do their best with the tools they are given.

Everyday Strategies to Build Planning and Prioritization Skills

Alexander Graham Bell once said, “Before anything else, preparation is the key to success.” Having the ability to plan and prioritize are important skills that we master over time. As adults, we zoom through the day and hardly notice the mental work we do. In fact, if someone were to ask how you balance it all, you may find it difficult to explain. I remember asking my mamaw once for the recipe to her chocolate pie. Her response? “I don’t really use a recipe. I just add what goes in it.” Much like my mamaw’s baking methods, we add a dash of this and a splash of that and usually arrive at a sweet and successful day.

Consider what your recipe to success is. Try writing down your routine and noticing what techniques you use to stay on schedule. Once you have a clear idea of your methods, bring them to your child’s attention. Invite your child to become a part of the “family planning committee” and provide visual reminders for them to use. For younger children or those with executive delays, picture charts will help them see the flow of their routine. Some children may prefer to use color coding while others may simply need a to-do list. Remember that they will need your help to continue sharpening their skills so offer prompts, reminders, and meaningful praise often!

IF, THEN

Before heading out the door, it's important to know where you're going in order to be prepared. In this next game, your child will practice preparing to go somewhere.

GOOD FOR: Planning and Prioritization, Working Memory, Impulse Control

MATERIALS:

Large bag
Paper
Pencil
Scissors
Variety of items that you would take to:
- A friend's house/ playdate
- A pool
- School
- A picnic

TIME NEEDED:
15 minutes

HELPFUL TIP:
For added fun, try this activity on a day when you truly have an outing planned. To increase the difficulty, have your child gather the items from various locations in the house. Add an extra challenge by saying, "Hurry, we're going to be late!" and giving your child a time limit.

INSTRUCTIONS:

1. Prepare the game by grabbing a few items that would be needed for each activity.
2. Spread the items out on a table or the floor.
3. Write each activity down on paper like this: "If I am going on a playdate with my friend, then I'll need . . ." Cut the activities out, then fold them so the words are hidden.
4. Show your child the items and explain that they would be used for different activities.
5. Tell them to pick a card and read it to them.
6. Ask them to choose which items they would need for the chosen activity. (Some items may be appropriate for more than one activity.)
7. Continue the game by returning the items to the table and choosing another card.

LET'S TALK ABOUT IT!

"What can we do to be the most prepared?" Talk about ways that planning can be made easier. (If a time limit was added): "Was it harder to focus with the time limit?" Talk about the pressure that limited time frames can add and explore how your child was able to work through that.

THE QUICKSAND GAME

In this fun and fast-paced game, your child will exercise their ability to plan and problem-solve as they try to get to the other side.

GOOD FOR: Planning and Prioritization, Impulse Control

MATERIALS:

Pillows, towels, and blankets
Timer (optional)

TIME NEEDED:
15 minutes

HELPFUL TIP:
Help your child create a strategy for the game by saying, "How will you get across without falling?" Get creative! Use other materials or increase the difficulty by adding rules like "Get the teddy to the other side" or "No hands allowed."

INSTRUCTIONS:

1. To prepare the game materials, fold the towels or blankets into squares.
2. Lay the pillows and folded items on the floor to create various "rocks" that your child will jump on. Try to space them close enough for your child to jump from one to the other.
3. Be sure to arrange them near soft furniture (couch, chair) to ensure safety.
4. Stack pillows or drape blankets and towels across furniture to create "barriers" that your child will need to crouch under or go around.
5. When the scene is set, explain to your child that they are in the desert and need to cross a pit of quicksand. If they touch the floor, they must go back and start over.
6. Optional: There's a sandstorm coming! Set a timer and have them race to the other side.

LET'S TALK ABOUT IT!

"What did you think about before crossing the quicksand?" Explore how planning ahead was helpful.

PICTURES TELL A STORY

When retelling a story, we use a variety of executive skills. For this activity, your child will use prioritization plus working memory to arrange details from a story in the correct order.

GOOD FOR: Planning and Prioritization, Working Memory

MATERIALS:

Children's book
Paper
Pencil
Crayons

TIME NEEDED:
15 minutes

HELPFUL TIP:
To increase the difficulty, consider adding more sections or using a longer story. If your child doesn't enjoy coloring, invite them to tell you the story from memory as you draw it.

INSTRUCTIONS:

1. First, read a short story to your child that would be easy to retell.
2. After finishing the story, use the pencil to divide the paper into five sections and label them 1 through 5.
3. Ask your child to retell the story using pictures. Explain that each space will have a picture that tells the story.
4. Invite your child to say each part of the story aloud and help them identify what to draw.
5. Once complete, have your child retell the story in sequence by using words such as "first," "then," and "finally."

LET'S TALK ABOUT IT!

"What happens if we rearrange the story?" Using the pictures, retell the story out of order. Talk about the importance of the story's sequence. Enjoy a good laugh with your child!

REWARDS FOR RESPONSIBILITIES

As you may have already discovered, positive reinforcement can help motivate your child to complete tasks. In this activity, they will enjoy a variety of rewards when they practice following a plan.

GOOD FOR: Planning and Prioritization, Impulse Control, Task Initiation

MATERIALS:

Paper
Pencil
Scissors
Glue
Cardboard (recycled from a cereal box or similar)
Crayons

TIME NEEDED:
15 minutes

HELPFUL TIP:
A great way to involve your child even more is by having them choose their own rewards.

LET'S TALK ABOUT IT!

"Did you notice that as the tasks got harder, the rewards got bigger?" Discuss how planning and following directions was important for the success of this task.

INSTRUCTIONS:

1. To start, you will need to identify at least five household chores that your child can do. The jobs should range from quick (feeding the fish) to time-consuming (cleaning their room). Number the tasks 1 through 5.
2. Write them on paper beginning with the easiest. Cut them out and glue to the cardboard in a horizontal row.
3. Write a reward for each task ranging from small (sticker) to big (trip to store). Cut them into strips.
4. Glue a small area of each reward strip to the bottom of the cardboard (so it dangles off the edge) under the coordinating task.
5. Provide these instructions: "Start with #1 and tear off the strip when it's done. Bring it to me for your reward! Then do #2, #3, and so on."
6. Each time your child completes a task, check their work. If more work is required, kindly ask that they complete the job.
7. Once the expectation is met, celebrate their achievement (even the small ones). Don't forget to reward them!

IN THE CLASSROOM

In this simple yet fun activity, your child will use their imagination and planning skills to create their version of a teacher's class schedule.

GOOD FOR: Planning and Prioritization, Working Memory

MATERIALS:

Paper
Pencil

TIME NEEDED:
15 minutes

HELPFUL TIP:
A great way to increase the connection with your child is to invest in their happiness. Consider going the extra mile and creating a mini DIY classroom.

INSTRUCTIONS:

1. Begin by inviting your child to play school.
2. Tell them they are the teacher and you are the student.
3. Their job is to create a classroom schedule that explains the routine for the day, then role-play what they would do as a teacher.
4. You may need to provide a few pointers, such as activities to start the day, lessons to teach, or how long to make each class.
5. Assist your child in creating the schedule. Allow them to do most of the work and only help if they ask.
6. If the schedule needs modifications, let your child know and explain why. ("I don't see a time for lunch. We'll need to take a break to eat. Where do you think we should add it?")
7. Follow your child's lead as they instruct you as your teacher. Fully commit to the play and try to have fun!

LET'S TALK ABOUT IT!

"What would class be like if your teacher didn't have a plan?" Explore this idea, focusing on the importance of having a plan.

WHAT'S THE GAME PLAN?

In this game, your child will race to find color-coded items around the house while sticking to the plan.

GOOD FOR: Planning and Prioritization, Sustained Attention and Goal-Oriented Persistence, Working Memory

MATERIALS:

Paper
Crayons
Basket or bag
5 items that are each: blue, red, yellow (blue hat, red toy fire truck, yellow ball)
Timer

TIME NEEDED:
10 minutes

HELPFUL TIP:
Consider turning this game into a relay race by using three people. Invite another family member to join the game and assign a color to each person.

INSTRUCTIONS:

1. To set up the game, hide all 15 items around the room.
2. Using the paper and crayons, write: *"Here's the GAME PLAN! Find these objects that are hidden around the room, beginning with number 1. As you find all of one color, bring them to me, then start finding the next color!"*
   a) *1: Blue*
   b) *2: Red*
   c) *3: Yellow*
3. Hand your child the instructions and explain the details.
4. Give them their basket and set the timer for 5 minutes.
5. Say, "Go!" and start the timer.
6. To win the game, your child will need to gather the objects correctly before the time runs out!

LET'S TALK ABOUT IT!

"Having a plan before we start a task can help us be successful." Discuss how grouping and prioritizing the colors ensured that we found all the objects—otherwise, we could have forgotten one.

LET'S BUILD A FORT

Creating a fort is a classic activity that requires many executive skills! In this exercise, your child will practice their ability to plan and prioritize as they create a cozy hangout.

GOOD FOR: Planning and Prioritization, Impulse Control

MATERIALS:

Paper
Pencil
A variety of blankets, sheets, towels, etc.
Clothespins, chip clips, or binder clips (optional)

TIME NEEDED:
15 minutes

HELPFUL TIP:
You could use clips or pins to secure the fort as needed. Once created, consider having a special snack or doing an activity together in their new hangout. Be sure to let your child know that the planning, gathering of materials, and creating a drawing are all part of the activity—don't let them skip this part!

INSTRUCTIONS:

1. Begin by determining where your child will build their fort. The area should have plenty of furniture to support the fort. Kitchen chairs work well.
2. Tell your child that you're going to work together to build a cool clubhouse. Help them make a list of what they'll need, then gather the materials.
3. Once they have everything together, say, "Okay, let's draw our design."
4. Allow your child to explore their thoughts and ideas for the fort. Sit down and help them create a drawing of their plan.
5. It's time to build! You may need to prompt them by saying, "What blankets will we use first?" or "Where should we start?"
6. Follow your child's lead until the fort is complete.

LET'S TALK ABOUT IT!

"Why did we draw a picture of your idea before we started building?" If your plans changed during building, discuss how and why things changed.

WANTS VS. NEEDS

An important strategy for children is to learn how to prioritize their needs versus their wants. In this activity, you will help your child identify their necessities and things that they can live without.

GOOD FOR: Planning and Prioritizing

MATERIALS:

Paper
Pencil
Highlighters or crayons

TIME NEEDED:
10 minutes

HELPFUL TIP:
Children are often passionate about their favorite things, and they may view their wants as necessities. Be sure to avoid ridiculing your child for their feelings. Instead, offer validation like this: "I know that you really love __________. Remember, necessities are things that our body requires to function, and you could live without ______________ if you had to."

INSTRUCTIONS:

1. Begin by asking your child, "What are some things that we need for survival?" Explore this topic and clarify that needs are the things our body has to have, whereas wants are things that make life more fun and enjoyable.
2. On the paper, have them make a list of their wants and needs. Try asking questions such as "What keeps your body working?" and "What are your favorite things?"
3. Once your child has completed their list, have them choose a color to use for wants and a color for needs.
4. Use the coordinating color to highlight or circle each item in the list.
5. Once complete, review the activity together. Explore your child's thoughts and feelings.

LET'S TALK ABOUT IT!

It's important that this activity is used as a guide and not a test. Be prepared as this may bring up worried thoughts in your child, which would be a normal response. Offer encouragement such as "It's hard to imagine life without our wants and hopefully that would never happen."

METEOROLOGIST FOR A DAY

One career that is centered around planning is meteorology, or the study of weather. In this activity, your child will harness their inner weatherperson as they predict the weather.

GOOD FOR: Planning and Prioritization, Working Memory

MATERIALS:

Paper
Pencil
Crayons

TIME NEEDED:
15 minutes

HELPFUL TIP:
Keep this activity going by having your child lay out their clothes according to tomorrow's weather.

INSTRUCTIONS:

1. Begin by helping your child do some weather research.
2. Using their paper, start by having your child write their forecast prediction for tomorrow. Details that could be included in their forecast predictions include air temperature, precipitation, humidity, sunrise/sunset time, and wind speed.
3. Using the crayons, have them include illustrations.
4. Repeat using the following day.
5. Once their weather forecast is complete, invite them to role-play, telling you about the forecast like a meteorologist on TV would do.

LET'S TALK ABOUT IT!

"Why is it important that we know the weather forecast for our area?" Discuss how using the weather prediction helps us dress appropriately, plan activities, etc.

RESCUE MISSION

Another set of careers that require the advanced ability to plan and prioritize are first responders. In this activity, your child will explore how they would respond to a minor emergency.

GOOD FOR: Planning and Prioritizing, Emotional Control

MATERIALS:

Item of your choice (that could get stuck in a tree or on a tall surface): kite, stuffed animal, ball, Frisbee, etc.
Paper
Pencil

TIME NEEDED:
10 minutes

HELPFUL TIP:
It's important that your child knows that asking for help is always a good option. Let them know that (if they didn't already) you are always willing to offer help. To avoid distress, be sure the object is something your child does not have an attachment to.

INSTRUCTIONS:

1. Begin by placing an object somewhere up high, being mindful of safety (in a tree, on a shelf). Be sure that it's visible.
2. Tell your child you need their help retrieving it.
3. Have them sit with their paper and pen to explore ideas of how they could get the object down. You can help them with ideas such as using a broom or a stool.
4. Once they have created their plan, help them act it out.

LET'S TALK ABOUT IT!

"If you came across a situation like this and you weren't at home, what would you do?" Discuss a few real-life scenarios at school or the park when your child may need to plan and prioritize to solve a problem. Reiterate that asking for an adult's help is always a great plan!

ON THE PAGE ACTIVITY

WHAT SHOULD YOU DO?

Often, children struggle to know when to act quickly and when the matter can wait. In this exercise, your child will evaluate scenarios and practice prioritizing urgent tasks. Have your child read through each scenario. Using a pencil, have them circle the star beside anything urgent, or the triangle if it's not.

1. You spilled a glass of water on the living room floor. ★ △
2. Someone is knocking at the door. ★ △
3. You want to tell your teacher a funny joke during class. ★ △
4. A friend asks you a question while you're taking a test. ★ △
5. You have incomplete homework that needs to be turned in tomorrow. ★ △
6. You see the pot of water on the stove is boiling over. ★ △
7. A strange grown-up speaks to you at the park. ★ △

8. You accidentally break your sister's toy when no one is looking.

9. Your parent is on the phone, but you are eager to tell them what you learned in science class.

HELPFUL TIP: Depending on your child's development, this exercise may be quite challenging. Consider talking through each scenario with them and helping them identify each scenario's level of urgency.

LET'S TALK ABOUT IT!

"Pick one of the 'star' situations and imagine if you didn't act quickly. What could happen?"

"Pick one of the 'triangle' situations and imagine if you acted too fast. What could happen?"

Discuss why it's important to know the difference between urgent and nonurgent.

A GARDEN OF GOALS

For this chapter's final activity, your child will explore their short- and long-term goals while designing their very own garden.

GOOD FOR: Planning and Prioritizing, Working Memory

MATERIALS:

Colored and plain paper
Scissors
Glue
Pencil
Crayons (optional)

TIME NEEDED:
15 minutes

HELPFUL TIP:
If your child is finding it difficult to grasp the meaning of short-term/long-term goals, try using seasons/grade levels as a frame of reference ("this summer" or "next year during fourth grade").

LET'S TALK ABOUT IT!

"When we set goals for the future, it's important that we know who will support us in achieving those goals."

"Who is your support system?"

INSTRUCTIONS:

1. Begin by helping your child create two large flowers:
   - Cut out two circles for each of the flowers' centers, ten ovals for each of their petals, and two slender rectangles for their stems.
2. On a plain sheet of paper, begin gluing the flowers together.
   - Each flower should have one center, five petals, and one stem.
3. Choose one flower to represent "long-term goals" and have the other represent "short-term goals."
4. Explain to your child that "short-term goals are things you want to accomplish soon, whereas long-term goals are things that you wish to achieve in the future."
5. Starting with the first flower, have your child write a short-term goal on each petal.
6. Next, move to the second flower, where you will have your child write their long-term goals on each petal.
7. Once they have written all their goals, invite your child to add more creative details to their garden (grass, sky, animals).

Key Takeaways

Helping your child improve their planning and prioritizing skills will create positive ripple effects for many years to come. Being prepared gives children the feeling of being in control, which leads to increased self-esteem and decreased anxiety. Learning to use a well-thought-out plan such as a chore chart offers the practice they need in a safe and supportive space.

- Almost every part of our day requires some level of planning and prioritizing.
- Although not every aspect of our lives is predictable, simply having a generalized idea provides the stability we need as human beings to thrive.
- Children need plenty of time and experience to effectively develop these skills.
- Invite your child to become a part of the "family planning committee" and provide visual reminders for them to use.
- Remember that they will need your help to continue sharpening their skills so offer prompts, reminders, and meaningful praise often!

CHAPTER 9

Get Organized

One of the executive skills that typically develops later is organization. For this reason, many children commonly struggle with sequencing and prioritizing tasks. Having a particular method for organization is important for many reasons. From maintaining a tidy space to managing our thoughts, this executive skill is a large contributor to our mental health. Organization is what human beings require both internally and externally to maintain a healthy rhythm and balance. In this chapter, you will find various games and activities specifically designed to help your child improve their organizational skills.

ORGANIZATION OVERHAUL

Grace was nine years old when she was referred for counseling by her pediatrician. She presented with persistent worry, anger outbursts, and low self-esteem. According to her parents, her symptoms were fairly new, seemingly starting overnight. Grace's parents reported that she was an excellent student who enjoys school; however, recently she had been complaining of frequent stomachaches and begging not to go to school in the mornings. Grace had been to see a gastroenterologist, who ruled out any medical issues.

Grace seemed to be putting an overwhelming amount of pressure on herself in school. She would make comments during the session such as "I'm the only one in my class who doesn't know how to do it." She discussed wanting to be "smart" like her friends and that she felt embarrassed at how many times she had to ask to borrow materials because she had lost hers. It became clear that Grace was giving her best effort but was still coming up short. This was an exhausting and demoralizing process.

A special teams meeting was held with Grace's teachers, parents, and counselors to discuss adding additional measures for academic support. Part of those measures included providing Grace with a "teacher mentor" who would check in with her periodically throughout the week to help her stay organized with materials and assignments. Within the first week of adding the accommodations, Grace's grades and attitude began to improve. By adding to her support system and giving her a moment to regroup, she was able to access the effective strategies needed to accomplish her goals.

Everyday Strategies to Build Organizational Skills

Implementing an organized system can be difficult to do. The problem isn't always a lack of skills, although that can be an issue in some cases. The challenge is the lack of time. You see, operating in an organized way is beneficial, but it's quite time-consuming, and as a parent your time is incredibly limited. Some of you will feel confident with moving forward in this chapter, but many of you may feel overwhelmed at the thought of organization.

Whether you are naturally tidy and neat or organization takes additional effort, please know that you have so much to offer your child. Organization requires the slowing down of the brain and body to effectively strategize a task. Expecting your child to be neat and clean is a lot to ask of their developing brain. Believe it or not, children actually crave structure and order; it's ingrained in their human nature. So, imagine the frustration when those around them view their messes as an intentional choice.

The key to helping your child build their organizational skills is to first validate their struggles. Let them know that you see and appreciate their effort. Be sure to actively involve them in your day-to-day strategies. This could mean implementing an afternoon activities checklist or having them help clean out the garage. Keep your expectations realistic. Remember that your child is doing their best with the brain that they have. As they are learning these new skills, offer consistent support and reminders to ensure they are set up for success.

TASTY AND COLORFUL ORGANIZATION

Let's start off our activities with a tasty treat, shall we? In this activity, your kiddo will surely be excited to practice their organization skills as they arrange their snack by colors.

GOOD FOR: Organization, Impulse Control

MATERIALS:

Multicolored candy pieces
Dinner plate

TIME NEEDED:
10 minutes

HELPFUL TIP:
Substitute food items with material items if needed, such as buttons, pom-poms, or pieces of paper. For an added challenge, have your child try using very small items, such as sprinkles.

INSTRUCTIONS:

1. For this game, you'll want to make sure you have a multicolored snack or candy on hand. (cereal, chocolate candies, fruit-flavored candies, gummy snacks.)
2. Have your child sit at a table with a plate in front of them (preferably white, so they can see the colored items better).
3. Instruct your child to create a rainbow with their goodies.
4. Clarify that just like when they draw a rainbow, each arch should be all the same color.
5. Once their rainbow is complete, they can eat!

LET'S TALK ABOUT IT!

"This activity was to help you practice organizing."
"How did you organize your rainbow?"
"What other things do you try to keep organized?"

ORGANIZATION CHAMPION!

In this find it–type game, your child will look for items that are out of place, then practice organization by returning them to where they go.

GOOD FOR: Organization, Impulse Control, Task Initiation

MATERIALS:

Household items (that are familiar to your child)
Timer

TIME NEEDED:
15 minutes

HELPFUL TIP:
Depending on your child's development, they may need more of your help during this activity. Give them a chance to try independently first, stepping in only if they seem to be stuck.

INSTRUCTIONS:

1. Begin by gathering five or more items that your child is familiar with (child's jacket, trash, toys, TV, etc.).
2. Distribute them around the room (on the floor, on furniture, or in containers), keeping them in plain sight.
3. Explain to your child that you're going to be playing a game where they find items that are "out of place" and return them to where they should go.
4. Set the timer for 5 minutes and say "Go!"
5. You may need to walk alongside them to help find where the item belongs.
6. As they put the items in their correct place, they will return to continue looking for items.
7. If they run out of time, no worries! Encourage them that they "are doing a great job" and start the timer over.
8. Once all items are in their correct places, your child has earned the title of organization champion! Celebrate their awesomeness!

LET'S TALK ABOUT IT!

> "Part of being a family means we can help each other stay organized. What can you do the next time you see something that is not where it's supposed to be?"

CLEANUP CHART CREATION

Children are most successful when they know exactly what the expectations are. In this activity, your child will have the opportunity to create a cleanup chart to help them gain more independence in their organizational abilities.

GOOD FOR: Organization, Working Memory, Task Initiation

MATERIALS:

Paper
Pencil
Crayons
Stickers (optional)

TIME NEEDED:
10 minutes

HELPFUL TIP:
If your child is more interested in getting up and playing during this activity, that is okay! Take the chart with you as you follow alongside them. Continue following the instructions to complete the activity as normal.

LET'S TALK ABOUT IT!

"This chart will help you keep your things more organized." Take this time to review the chart with your child and walk them through the motions.

INSTRUCTIONS:

1. Begin by sitting down with your child and asking, "What does it mean when I ask you to clean up?"
2. Explore the process for putting away their toys and explain that written reminders can help us be successful.
3. Say, "To help you in cleaning up your toys, we are going to create your own cleanup chart!"
4. Help your child get started by writing the title "[child's name]'s Cleanup Chart."
5. Following your child's lead, begin exploring what toys or items they usually play with the most. You could say, "Tell me about some of your favorite toys here at home."
6. Now it's time to draw! Help your child draw and color pictures that represent each toy they will need to put away.
7. Once complete, help your child hang their new chart in a place they commonly play, such as their bedroom or playroom. Invite them to try it out and reward them with a sticker.

CHAIN OF MANY COLORS

Organization creates more predictability in our lives, which is especially good for our mental health. In this activity, your child will create a pattern as they make a paper chain.

GOOD FOR: Attention to Detail and Frustration Tolerance, Organization

MATERIALS:

Colored paper (or plain)
Crayons (if using plain paper)
Scissors
Tape

TIME NEEDED:
10 minutes

HELPFUL TIP:
For added difficulty, prompt your child to make a more challenging pattern to complete. Invite them to choose a place in the house to hang up their beautiful paper chain!

INSTRUCTIONS:

1. Begin by cutting the paper into strips.
2. If using plain white paper, have your child color the strips of paper various solid colors.
3. Once there are at least 10 strips of paper, it's time to create the chain!
4. Have your child look at the colors and decide what pattern they would like to create.
5. Help them make a loop with a paper strip and secure it with tape. (It should look like a circle.)
6. Choose the next colored strip and thread it through the paper loop. Bring the ends together and secure with tape. Remind your child to maintain the pattern.
7. Continue this process until all the strips have been used.

LET'S TALK ABOUT IT!

"Why do patterns help us stay more organized?" Discuss how it can be helpful to know what is coming next.

SOCKS ON THE FLOOR, SOCKS GALORE!

In this super silly game, your child will practice their organization skills while doing a little laundry. (You're welcome!)

GOOD FOR: Organization, Impulse Control, Working Memory

MATERIALS:

Several clean pairs of socks
Timer

TIME NEEDED:
15 minutes

HELPFUL TIP:
Add a musical component to the game by stopping and starting the music instead of using a timer.

INSTRUCTIONS:

1. Begin by gathering several pairs of clean, matching socks from around the house
2. Tell your child that you're going to show them a fun way to do laundry!
3. Make a pile of the socks on the floor. Make sure they are mixed up well.
4. Setting the timer for 1 minute, tell your child to begin looking for matches.
5. As they find matching pairs, set them aside.
6. When the time is up, your child must wear whatever sock they are holding on their feet or hands.
7. Continue with the game, resetting the timer each round, until your child has found all the matches.

LET'S TALK ABOUT IT!

"Organization doesn't have to be boring. Can you think of some other ways that we could make organizing fun?"

ORGANIZE FOR A CAUSE

Part of staying organized means decluttering when items are not being used. In this activity, your child will practice altruism along with organization as they consider donating toys that they no longer want.

GOOD FOR: Organization, Task Initiation

MATERIALS:

Trash bag or box
Marker

TIME NEEDED:
15 minutes

HELPFUL TIP:
Encourage your child's ability to let go of things they no longer use by modeling this behavior yourself. Consider creating your own box of things to give away.

INSTRUCTIONS:

1. Before starting this activity, consider sitting with your child and reading a book, watching a video, or telling a story about giving.
2. Grab a trash bag or box and begin helping your child identify items (toys, clothes, games) that they no longer use.
3. Consider creating a reward system for your child to earn a special incentive for every item they donate. (1 item = 1 point, 10 points = trip to get ice cream.)
4. Once the bag/box is full, have your child write or draw a special message to the person who will receive the items.
5. Arrange a special day to give your child their reward when you drop off the donations.

LET'S TALK ABOUT IT!

"Staying organized isn't always easy, especially when we have a lot of stuff."

"How did it feel to give away some of your things?"

"Did you notice any uncomfortable emotions once you saw that the items were gone?"

Discuss their feelings throughout the activity and share your feelings as well.

FISHING FOR COLORS

In this fun game, your child will fish for shapes and work on organizing them by color.

GOOD FOR: Organization, Impulse Control

MATERIALS:

DIY MINIATURE FISHING POLE:

A long object (ruler, wooden spoon, chopstick, etc.)
String
Scissors
Tape

FISH SHAPES:

Paper (construction or plain)
Crayons
Scissors

TIME NEEDED:
15 minutes

HELPFUL TIP:
Increase the difficulty (and the fun) by having your child spin around five times before their next turn!

INSTRUCTIONS:

1. First, work with your child to create their miniature fishing pole. Measure the string to be slightly longer than the "pole," cut it, and tie it to the end. Attach a piece of tape (folded sticky-side out) to the tip of the string.
2. Now your child will create their fish shapes. Have them draw various small shapes and add a "fish face" to each. The fish shapes should be various colors. If you are using white paper, have your child color them. Cut out each fish shape and spread them out on the table.
3. Time to play! Have your child "fish" for shapes with their fishing pole. Holding the pole, dangle the string above a fish and try to stick it with the tape.
4. Once they catch one, they will remove it and place it in a pile, separating each fish shape by its color. (Reattach the tape if necessary, or replace with a new piece of tape.)
5. Win the game by catching all the fish and organizing them by color.

LET'S TALK ABOUT IT!

"In this game, we were organizing the fish by colors. What is another way we could have organized the fish?"

ORGANIZED ART

In this activity, your child will use mindfulness and art to practice organizing their thoughts as they paint a meaningful picture.

GOOD FOR: Organization, Task Initiation, Emotional Control

MATERIALS:

Paper
Cup of water
Paintbrushes
Paint

TIME NEEDED:
10 minutes

HELPFUL TIP:
For even more organized thinking, have your child make a list of ideas for their painting before they get started.

INSTRUCTIONS:

1. Start by preparing the materials for the activity, including the paper, a cup of water with paintbrushes, and paint.
2. Explain to your child that this activity is to help them organize their thoughts. Ask them to paint whatever comes to mind.
3. After a few minutes, sit with your child to discuss their picture. Have them explain their thoughts and inspiration.
4. Once it dries, have your child choose a special place to hang their masterpiece!

LET'S TALK ABOUT IT!

> "It's important that our mind is organized just like our home. When we stop to think before completing an activity, it can help us do our best work." This is another opportunity to bring up nonjudgmental awareness or mindfulness, and practice noticing their thoughts.

AFTER-SCHOOL CHECKLIST

A great way to stay organized is through using a checklist. For the next activity, your child will create an after-school chart to help them effectively organize their afternoon tasks.

GOOD FOR: Organization, Task Initiation, Working Memory

MATERIALS:

Paper
Scissors
Pencil
Art supplies (optional)

TIME NEEDED:
10 minutes

HELPFUL TIP:
Once a checklist is made, the key is remembering to use it! You can help support your child in staying organized by directing them to their checklist when they have missed a task.

INSTRUCTIONS:

1. First, have your child cut their paper longways down the center.
2. Have them write their checklist title such as "My After-School Activities" on one half.
3. A second piece of paper can be used to brainstorm (or write down ideas).
4. Discuss the various expectations for your child when they get home (extracurriculars, homework, household chores).
5. Take this time to also explore your child's wants and needs in the afternoon (quiet time, a healthy snack, screen time, one-on-one time with a parent).
6. Now help your child create their after-school checklist, combining parent expectations with your little one's wants and needs.
7. Invite your child to add creative details if they wish.

LET'S TALK ABOUT IT!

"Now that you have a checklist to help you stay organized, it will be important for you to remember to use it." Talk about ways to make this method more effective such as posting the checklist somewhere visible.

VISUAL REMINDERS

Children often need frequent prompts to complete tasks. In this activity, your child will learn about creating their own visual reminders to help them get things done.

GOOD FOR: Organization, Task Initiation

MATERIALS:

Sticky notes or pieces of paper with tape
Pencil

TIME NEEDED:
10 minutes

HELPFUL TIP:
Your child will likely need your help to recognize the tasks that they typically forget. Be supportive and encouraging as you remind them of these ideas.

INSTRUCTIONS:

1. Start by explaining to your child that sometimes we forget things, and that is completely normal.
2. Discuss methods of organization, such as to-do lists and calendars, which can help us complete tasks. Explain that having visual reminders can be helpful as well.
3. Tell your child that they are going to create their own visual reminders.
4. Using the sticky notes or pieces of paper, have your child write short reminders that would be helpful (brush your teeth, take out the trash, put dirty clothes in laundry).
5. Have them post the reminders somewhere that they look daily (bathroom mirror).

LET'S TALK ABOUT IT!

"Now that we have created your reminders, think about other times where you have seen people use visual reminders like these." Discuss ways that you, their teacher, or others write notes and post reminders to help with daily tasks.

THE ORGANIZATION CHALLENGE

Children with advanced executive skills tend to have more capabilities with organization than younger kids do. In this game, your child's organizational skills will be put to the test as they complete various challenges.

GOOD FOR: Organization, Task Initiation, Working Memory

MATERIALS:

Paper
Scissors
Pencil
Timer

TIME NEEDED:
15 minutes

HELPFUL TIP:
This game would be a blast to play with a group. Invite siblings, family members, or friends to play along. If your child seems overly challenged by a task, have them say "pass" to exchange their card.

INSTRUCTIONS:

1. First, create the task cards by cutting squares of paper and writing down tasks that your child could reasonably perform in 3 minutes.
   - Examples of tasks: unload five items from dishwasher, fold five pieces of laundry and put away, take out trash, feed pet, tidy their shoes, throw away trash from bedroom.
2. On the back of each task card, write the reward for completing that task.
   - Examples: money, candy, screen time.
3. Lay the task cards, reward-side up, on the table and tell your child to choose one.

4. Explain to your child that they will race to complete organizational tasks. If they complete it fast, they will earn a reward. Set the timer for 3 minutes and give your child the cue to start.
5. If they complete the task in time, they keep the card.
6. If they run out of time, they simply return the card to the table and try again.
7. Continue the game until all the tasks are complete or your child is ready to stop.

LET'S TALK ABOUT IT!

> "You did a fantastic job with this game!"
>
> "Each of the tasks help us as a family maintain an organized home."
>
> Discuss various aspects of your household system for organization and why they are important.

ON THE PAGE ACTIVITY

LET'S JOURNAL!

Organization extends beyond the space around us and is necessary to ensure we remain emotionally healthy. For this activity, your child will practice organizing their thoughts and feelings as they complete a series of journal prompts. Read these prompts with your child and record their answers.

1. Today, I feel ______________ because ______________________.
2. Something that made me feel stressed today was ______________________.
3. When I feel stressed or unhappy, ______________ makes me feel better.
4. Something that made me laugh today was ______________________.
5. A teacher or coach once told me ______________ and I felt really proud!
6. I am thankful because ______________________.
7. I am still learning how to ______________________.
8. An activity that makes me feel calm is ______________________.
9. Someday, I hope to achieve ______________________.
10. Two things that my friends love about me are:

    ______________________________________ and

    ______________________________________.

LET'S TALK ABOUT IT!

"Did you know that you just did an organizational exercise for your mind?"

Explore the benefits of journaling and offer incentives such as purchasing a new notebook or fancy pen if they incorporate it into their daily routine.

Key Takeaways

It can be difficult to know how much to expect of your child's abilities. When it comes to organization, it's an advanced skill that will likely take time for your child to master. Having effective strategies in place at home will help your child to see organization in action. Be patient and willing to adapt strategies to their needs. What is helpful for you may not be what is helpful to them. Try to maintain a positive mindset and take the time to understand your child's perspective.

- Organization is what human beings require both internally and externally to maintain a healthy rhythm and balance.
- Maintaining a particular order is beneficial, but it's quite time-consuming and as a parent your time is incredibly limited.
- Expecting your child to be neat and clean is a lot to ask of their developing brain.
- Remember that your child is doing their best.
- As they are learning these new skills, offer consistent support and reminders to ensure they are set up for success.

CHAPTER 10

Stay Flexible

Life is unpredictable and even the most prepared and organized person can be caught off guard. When life gives us lemons, we can make lemonade, but only if we have the right ingredients. Cognitive flexibility is the sugar that makes life's sour moments a bit more bearable. It's the skill that allows us to adjust to change and overcome adversity. With flexibility being one of the last executive skills to develop, many children have limited mental flexibility that can appear as emotional or behavioral issues. In this final chapter, you will walk alongside your child as they strengthen their resilience and become flexible thinkers.

THE IMPORTANCE OF VALIDATION

Ella was seven years old when she was initially brought to therapy. Her dad reported that she had been struggling with anxiety for the past year. He explained that Ella "worries about everything" and "freaks out" anytime something doesn't go her way. He gave the example of a time that Ella's older sister had a minor sports injury that required the family to go to the emergency room. The next day, Ella was so upset that they had missed their weekly family movie night that she "screamed and cried for two hours." Her dad was insightful about Ella's mom moving out of state, saying that she seemed to only care about buying the kids' affection with gifts. During her sessions, Ella's demeanor was usually pleasant and positive. She talked without hesitation about her experiences with her mom and was insightful into her feelings of anger and sadness. Ella explained that she was tired of the plans changing. She felt that her dad didn't care about her feelings, and this made it difficult for her to open up to him. Instead, Ella would bottle up her emotions, leading to more rigid thinking and less flexibility. Through weekly therapy sessions, Ella learned to feel more empowered and in control. Ella's dad gained a better understanding of her perception and learned how to offer her a more validating and supportive environment. With these positive changes in place, Ella was able to maintain emotional control much more frequently.

Everyday Strategies to Build Mental Flexibility

Many people tend to think of kids as passengers on a boat who are along for the voyage. Instead, we should view children as the captains of their own ships and equip them with the ability to navigate life's choppy waters. Although their own mental flexibility will not fully mature for many more years, your child has the capacity to learn from you. Lessons are best learned when they can be both practiced and observed. Without a doubt, life will always be full of surprises, and you can use those opportunities to model adaptability and positivity. For instance, the next time there's a change in plans, mention how you're using mental flexibility to get through the situation. Try teaching your child how to prepare for unforeseen circumstances by creating a "rainy day fund" together.

Proactive strategies are helpful in the moment, but preventive measures are just as important. Mental flexibility is only a short-term solution and must be paired with emotional control skills to ensure the body can return to proper functioning. This could look like taking a moment to breathe deeply and check in with yourself or writing in a journal. As your child sees you are using these healthy strategies, they will be more likely to use similar skills for themselves when plans need to change.

BENDING THE RULES

Children tend to dislike rules and view them as unimportant. In this activity, your child will use flexible thinking as they play a game without the usual set of requirements.

GOOD FOR: Flexibility, Impulse Control, Working Memory, Task Initiation

MATERIALS:

Board game, deck of cards, dice, etc.

TIME NEEDED:
15 minutes

HELPFUL TIP:
To increase the challenge, you may choose to omit more than one rule. You could even try playing without any rules!

INSTRUCTIONS:

1. Begin by having your child choose a game of their choice. This could be a board game, card game, tag, hide-and-seek, etc.
2. Before getting started, add a twist by removing one important rule from the game.
3. Play the game as usual, ensuring that the chosen rule is omitted. Continue playing until someone wins!

LET'S TALK ABOUT IT!

"What did you think about the game when we changed it?" "Was it as fun with fewer rules?" Take a moment to discuss how this activity required your child to be flexible.

FLEXIBILITY TRUTH OR DARE

In this daring game, your child will be challenged to use flexible thinking as they choose to answer a question or try something new.

GOOD FOR: Flexibility, Emotional Control

MATERIALS:

Items for dares (slice of lemon for new food experience or hair gel for a wacky hairstyle)
Dice

TIME NEEDED:
15 minutes

HELPFUL TIP:
For "truth," ask your child questions about new experiences, such as "If you went to a restaurant that only had foods you've never tried, what would you do?" or "If you joined a new sports team and didn't know any of your teammates, how would you make friends?"

INSTRUCTIONS:

1. First, you will need to prepare a few "dares" for the game. These should be experiences that are new to your child, such as tasting a new food, wearing a different hairstyle, or feeling a strange texture.
2. To start the game, your child will roll the dice. Even numbers mean you can ask them a question and they must tell the truth. Odd numbers mean they do a dare.
3. When your child rolls a dare, give them two choices of a new experience that you dare them to try.
4. Continue the game until each dare has been tried or offered.

LET'S TALK ABOUT IT!

"Being flexible helps us try new things!" Talk about how it's important to challenge ourselves sometimes.

WACKY COLORING

In this creative and wacky activity, your child will exercise their mental flexibility as they think outside the box to color a picture.

GOOD FOR: Flexibility, Impulse Control, Working Memory, Task Initiation

MATERIALS:

Paper
Pencil
Crayons

TIME NEEDED:
10 minutes

HELPFUL TIP:
This activity may be challenging for some children. Try to avoid pushing or forcing the activity. Instead, encourage your child to create a picture of nature that is "wacky and fun."

INSTRUCTIONS:

1. Begin by telling your child to imagine the colors of the outdoors. Ask them to describe what colors come to mind.
2. Now challenge them to create a picture where they use different colors for things in nature (for instance, a forest with pink trees, a soccer field with blue grass, or a farm with multicolored animals).
3. Throughout the activity, allow your child independent work time to create their own unique ideas. Offer support when needed.

LET'S TALK ABOUT IT!

"It can be hard and even uncomfortable to think about things in a different way. Was this activity hard or easy for you?" This is a great starting point to gauge your child's comfort level with flexible thinking.

I'VE GOT THIS!

For a child, adapting to a new situation can be hard work with little reward. For this activity, you will help motivate your child to practice mental flexibility by creating a reward chart together.

GOOD FOR: Flexibility, Organization

MATERIALS:

Paper
Pencil
Crayons
Stickers (optional)

TIME NEEDED:
15 minutes

HELPFUL TIP:
Consider placing a sticker beside the behavior each time it is used to offer a visual reminder of your child's achievements!

LET'S TALK ABOUT IT!

"Sometimes it's hard to be a positive thinker, especially when we're having a bad day." Talk about a time when plans had to change and validate your child's feelings. "Which of the positive behaviors from your chart could have been helpful?"

INSTRUCTIONS:

1. Begin by sitting with your child and exploring situations where mental flexibility would be helpful (rainy day, substitute teacher, losing a game).
2. Discuss what being flexible would look like in these scenarios: "How could we make the best out of the situation?"
3. Number 1 through 5 on a piece of paper and list the following positive behaviors:
    - "Able to find the good in the situation"
    - "Takes a deep breath to stay calm"
    - "Talks about their feelings"
    - "Goes with the flow when plans change"
    - "Asks for help"
4. Invite your child to decorate their chart with "flexible" designs like scribbles and swirls.
5. Hang it up on the refrigerator or a commonly used area and acknowledge when your child is able to use them.

OPPOSITE DAY

What better way to practice being flexible than to have an opposite day? For this activity, your child will imagine what their day would consist of if they did everything in the opposite way.

GOOD FOR: Flexibility, Task Initiation, Working Memory

MATERIALS:

Paper
Pencil

TIME NEEDED:
10 minutes

HELPFUL TIP:
Become the "coolest parent on the block" by bringing your child's opposite day to life! Set a date for the family to follow along with your child's plans. For a quick and easier option, try having an "opposite hour" to allow your child to briefly play out their opposite day ideas.

INSTRUCTIONS:

1. First, ask your child to think about what a day would be like if everything was the opposite. (How would our clothes look? How would we walk or talk? How would we eat?)
2. Now tell your child to write a plan for an opposite day for their family. Ask them to include the details of the day, such as no means yes, clothes on backward, or anything else that should be done differently.
3. Once the list is created, invite your child to try out some of their opposite day ideas.

LET'S TALK ABOUT IT!

"It sounds super silly and fun, but do you think it may be hard to do everything the opposite way?" "Why?" Discuss how mental flexibility would be important to do things differently.

FLEXIBLE OR FIRM?

Children learn best when they can engage their senses. In this activity, you help them understand flexibility by allowing them to feel it.

GOOD FOR: Flexibility

MATERIALS:

Flexible items (playdough or slime, stuffed animal, pillow)
Firm items (rock, pencil, plastic building bricks or blocks)
Blanket

TIME NEEDED:
15 minutes

HELPFUL TIP:
To help your child connect the deeper meaning, ask them to give an example of someone being flexible or firm. If your child seems to have difficulty understanding the underlying meaning, you can give them some of your own examples.

INSTRUCTIONS:

1. Before you begin, set up the flexible and firm items on a table. Cover the items with the blanket.
2. Invite your child to sit at the table.
3. Explain that flexibility means able to change or be made different, whereas firm means hard or rigid and unable to be changed.
4. Have your child reach under the blanket and feel each different object. Ask them to identify whether the object is flexible or firm.

LET'S TALK ABOUT IT!

"It's important to point out that both of these traits can be beneficial." Talk about when it would be helpful for someone to be firm, such as a teacher or coach.

FOLLOW THE FLEXIBLE LEADER

It's Simon Says with a flexible twist! In this game, your child will identify the thoughts and behaviors of someone who is adapting through change.

GOOD FOR: Flexibility, Working Memory, Impulse Control

MATERIALS:

None

TIME NEEDED:
10 minutes

HELPFUL TIP:
This game would be even better with a group of people. Invite a few more people to play for extra fun.

INSTRUCTIONS:

1. For this game, you will say, "A flexible thinker . . ." and choose to say either a true or false statement.
    a) . . . can't stop thinking about the way things used to be.
    b) . . . is positive.
    c) . . . can plan ahead.
    d) . . . is always happy.
2. Instruct your child that if they think it's true, they should give a thumbs-up. If they think it's not true, give a thumbs-down.
3. If your child gets it wrong, they should do a few stretches (to help them become more flexible, of course!). If they get it right, give them a small reward, such as one M&M for each correct answer.
4. Continue the game for several rounds.

LET'S TALK ABOUT IT!

> "Why do you think it would be helpful to think positively in a difficult situation?" Talk with your child about the power of positive thinking and how it can change the way we feel.

RAINY DAY FUN

Rainy days often interfere with plans and take away the fun. In this activity, your child will be challenged to change their perspective and imagine the fun that could be had when the weather isn't cooperating.

GOOD FOR: Flexibility, Planning and Prioritization

MATERIALS:

Paper
Pencil

TIME NEEDED:
10 minutes

HELPFUL TIP:

Throughout this activity, keep an open dialogue about your child's emotions. Flexibility is typically coupled with feelings such as disappointment and frustration. It's important for your child to voice these discomforts.

INSTRUCTIONS:

1. Start by prompting your child to think of a time when the weather ruined their plans. (Have an example in mind in case your child gets stuck.) Discuss how this made them feel.
2. Now explore how mental flexibility could be helpful when the weather causes plans to change. Say, "We can make the best out of the situation if we have the right mindset!"
3. Instruct your child to make a list of activities and ideas for future rainy days.
4. Help them with ideas that may take place at home or somewhere else. This could include baking cookies, doing an art activity, or going to the movies.

LET'S TALK ABOUT IT!

"I'm excited that we have some great ideas together for the next rainy day!" Discuss how the rainy day activities may not be as exciting as the originally planned event but will hopefully provide a bit of fun in the meantime.

"Do you remember the time when ________________ kept us from doing/going to ______________ but we still got to do it later?" Talk about how plans can sometimes just be delayed versus cancelled to help your child remain trusting and hopeful for future flexible moments.

SWITCH IT UP

If you've ever tried to write with your nondominant hand, then you know it's a difficult task. For this activity, your child will be challenged to use their flexibility skills as they try to write with their opposite hand.

GOOD FOR: Flexibility

MATERIALS:

Paper
Pencil
Crayons

TIME NEEDED:
10 minutes

HELPFUL TIP:
Keep in mind that your child has been using their dominant hand for many years now. Offer reminders throughout this activity for your child to use the opposite hand.

INSTRUCTIONS:

1. First, explain to your child the reason behind this activity. Talk about the difficulty of writing with your opposite hand and the importance of flexibility.
2. Using the opposite hand only, have your child draw or color a picture.
3. Next, try another everyday activity such as getting dressed or eating. Remind your child that they can only use their opposite hand.

LET'S TALK ABOUT IT!

"There are rare occasions where we may need to use a backup plan, such as our nondominant hand, to complete a task." Discuss how thinking and practicing the skill of mental flexibility in advance would help them prepare for moments of disappointment if they arise.

ROLL THE DICE, MAKE IT TWICE

For this game, your child will practice their math skills and mental flexibility as they create multiple products from the same number.

GOOD FOR: Flexibility, Working Memory

MATERIALS:

Dice
Small objects for counting (buttons, stones, beads, candies, macaroni)

TIME NEEDED:
10 minutes

HELPFUL TIP:
To increase the difficulty, double the amount rolled or use more dice to create a bigger number.

INSTRUCTIONS:

1. Set up the game by laying out the dice and small objects.
2. Explain to your child that they will roll the dice, then find two ways to create the number (rolls a 5; separates objects into groups of 1 and 4, then 3 and 2).
3. Tell your child to begin. Encourage them to talk you through their strategy.
4. Continue the game for several rounds.

LET'S TALK ABOUT IT!

"When we consider multiple options to achieve the same result, that's using our mental flexibility skills."

"What are some other times when you have thought about doing things differently?"

CHANGE FOR POSITIVE CHOICES

Change is hard, and it can help your child to stay motivated by using positive reinforcement. In this activity, you will work with your child to create a system to reward their flexibility.

GOOD FOR: Flexibility, Emotional Control

MATERIALS:

Paper
Scissors
Pencil
Coins (quarters)
Tape

TIME NEEDED:
10 minutes

HELPFUL TIP:
Although you may have already defined mental flexibility, go ahead and explain the idea to your child again. This will ensure that they are set up for success with this activity.

INSTRUCTIONS:

1. First, you will work with your child to create a coin chart.
2. Cut a strip of paper longways and divide into sections using the pencil.
3. Place a coin in each section and secure with tape.
4. Hang the coin chart somewhere visible.
5. Discuss with your child that you want to see them use mental flexibility. To help motivate them, you're offering a coin for each time they display this skill.
6. In the coming days, catch them using flexible thinking and instruct them to take a coin for their efforts.

LET'S TALK ABOUT IT!

"What are some examples of flexible thinking that you could set as your goal for this week?" You may need to offer a few examples for your child to choose from.

ON THE PAGE ACTIVITY

SPOT THE FLEXIBLE THOUGHTS

This activity will help your child spot the flexible thinking styles in communication and behavior. Have your child read the following statements and check off the ones that use flexible thinking.

- ☐ "I've got this."
- ☐ "This is the worst day ever."
- ☐ "I will make the best of the situation."
- ☐ "I can't do this."
- ☐ "Change is tough, but so am I."
- ☐ "There's nothing good that will come from this."
- ☐ "I didn't want this to happen."
- ☐ "Nothing good ever happens to me."
- ☐ "Everything will be okay."
- ☐ "This will still be a great day."

HELPFUL TIP: For the inflexible thoughts, have your child try to turn them into more helpful thoughts.

LET'S TALK ABOUT IT!

"What is good about having a positive attitude?"

"How might flexible thinking help us when our plans change?"

TRUST ME

In this game, your child will use flexibility as they navigate their surroundings using only the directions that you give them.

GOOD FOR: Flexibility

MATERIALS:

Cloth

TIME NEEDED:
15 minutes

HELPFUL TIP:
Increase the difficulty by placing small obstacles for your child to blindly maneuver around.

INSTRUCTIONS:

1. First, designate the area that you will use for this activity and identify the starting point and finish line.
2. Tell your child that to win the game, they simply have to walk from "here" to "there"—but blindfolded.
3. Let your child know that you will be giving them directions of where to walk and turn. Say, "You must listen closely and trust me to guide you."
4. Begin the game by putting the blindfold over your child's eyes. Give your child specific instructions to help them cross the room (walk three steps forward, turn right, step over).
5. The challenge is complete when they can reach the other side of the room!

LET'S TALK ABOUT IT!

"When we set goals for the future, it's important that we know who will support us in achieving those goals."

"Who is your support system?"

"How do you build trust with others?"

Key Takeaways

Mental flexibility offers kids and adults alike the opportunity to look on the bright side of things and find the good in any situation. When children are empowered to look within for a solution, they realize that they have more control over their life than they thought.

- When life gives us lemons, we can make lemonade only if we have the right ingredients. Although not every aspect of our lives is predictable, simply having a generalized idea provides the stability we need as human beings to thrive.
- Cognitive flexibility is the sugar that makes life's sour moments a bit more bearable.
- With flexibility being one of the last executive skills to develop, many children have limited mental flexibility that can appear as emotional or behavioral issues.
- Mental flexibility is only a short-term solution and must be paired with emotional control skills to ensure the body can return to proper functioning.

CLOSING THOUGHTS

Woo-hoo, you completed the book! Take a moment to acknowledge the commitment and dedication that it took to tackle this project. There was no formal obligation, yet you stuck with it for your child. That is part of what makes you a great parent!

When you stop to consider the executive functioning processes, it can help you realize the great need for these skills in children of all ages. Executive functioning is vital for your child's success in the classroom, at home, and beyond. From safely walking in a busy parking lot to the ability to solve a math problem, these abilities are crucial for everyday life.

Moving forward, remember the strategies that your child seemed to connect with the most and try to use them whenever possible. Avoid being critical or passing judgment. Instead, be mindful of your child's needs and be available to offer your support. Consider creating a "skills box" with a variety of "tools" for your child to use, such as fidgets and sensory items. If your child seems to regress in their executive skills down the road, simply pull the workbook back out and do a short review. Remember to use the power of positivity and praise to keep your child motivated. Take note of the areas in which you hope to continue improving and allow yourself plenty of grace.

Remember that kids will do their best with the tools that they are given. Above all else, find ways to emotionally connect with your child. Sit and listen intently to their thoughts and experiences, pencil in time to spend together, and allow them to take the lead every now and then.

RESOURCES

Websites

ADDitudeMag.com
ADDitude Magazine and website immerses readers with rich, scientific information about living a fulfilling life following a diagnosis of ADHD.

BigLifeJournal.com
Big Life Journal is an online company offering a variety of resources and tools that encourage executive functioning skills in children.

ChildMind.org
Child Mind Institute is a website offering education and resources on childhood mental health.

PsychologyToday.com/us
Psychology Today offers an easy way to search for local mental health providers in your area.

Podcasts

ADHD Parenting
This podcast offers families a complete wraparound of support as they navigate the triumphs and challenges of raising a neurodivergent child.

Books

A Little SPOT series by Diane Alber
This is a collection of books that aim to teach children valuable life skills while inspiring their creativity.

***Different: A Great Thing to Be!* by Heather Avis and Sarah Mensinga**
This *New York Times* bestseller is a short story geared toward younger children about embracing their uniqueness and appreciating the differences in others.

REFERENCES

Arain, Mariam, Maliha Haque, Lina Johal, Puja Mathur, Wynand Nel, Afsha Rais, and Sushil Sharma. "Maturation of the Adolescent Brain." *Neuropsychiatric Disease and Treatment* 9 (2013): 449–461. doi.org/10.2147/NDT.S39776.

Corbett, Blythe A., Laura J. Constantine, Robert Hendren, David Rocke, and Sally Ozonoff. "Examining Executive Functioning in Children with Autism Spectrum Disorder, Attention Deficit Hyperactivity Disorder and Typical Development." *Psychiatry Research* 166, nos. 2–3 (April 2009): 210–222. doi.org/10.1016/j.psychres.2008.02.005.

Frankel, Leslie A., Sheryl O. Hughes, Teresia M. O'Connor, Thomas G. Power, Jennifer O. Fisher, and Nancy L. Hazen. "Parental Influences on Children's Self-Regulation of Energy Intake: Insights from Developmental Literature on Emotion Regulation." *Journal of Obesity* 2012 (March 2012): 327259. doi.org/10.1155/2012/327259.

Fredrickson, Barbara L. "The Role of Positive Emotions in Positive Psychology: The Broaden-and-Build Theory of Positive Emotions." *American Psychologist* 56, no. 3 (March 2001): 218–226. doi.org/10.1037/0003-066X.56.3.218.

Gavit, Oana Alexandra, Daniel David, Raymond DiGiuseppe, and Tamara DelVecchio. "The Development and Validation of the Parent Rational and Irrational Beliefs Scale." *Procedia—Social and Behavioral Sciences* 30 (2011): 2305–2311. doi.org/10.1016/j.sbspro.2011.10.449.

Holmes, Joni, Susan E. Gathercole, Maurice Place, Darren L. Dunning, Kerry A. Hilton, and Julian G. Elliott. "Working Memory Deficits Can Be Overcome: Impacts of Training and Medication on Working Memory in Children with ADHD." *Applied Cognitive Psychology* 24, no. 6 (September 2010): 827–836. doi.org/10.1002/acp.1589.

National Institute of Mental Health. "Attention-Deficit/Hyperactivity Disorder." Last modified September 2021. nimh.nih.gov/health/topics/attention-deficit-hyperactivity-disorder-adhd.

Phelan, Ruth F., Deborah J. Howe, Emma L. Cashman, and Samantha H. Batchelor. "Enhancing Parenting Skills for Parents with Mental Illness: The Mental Health Positive Parenting Program." *Medical Journal of Australia* 199, no. 3 (October 2013): 30–33. doi.org/10.5694/mja11.11181.

van der Donk, Martha L. A., Anne-Claire Hiemstra-Beernink, Ariane C. Tjeenk-Kalff, Aryan V. van der Leij and Ramón J. L. Lindauer. "Interventions to Improve Executive Functioning and Working Memory in School-Aged Children with AD(H)D: A Randomised Controlled Trial and Stepped-Care Approach." *BMC Psychiatry* 13, no. 23 (January 2013). doi.org/10.1186/1471-244X-13-23.

Wolraich, Mark L., Joseph F. Hagan Jr., Carla Allan, Eugenia Chan, Dale Davison, Marian Earls, Steven W. Evans, et al. "Clinical Practice Guideline for the Diagnosis, Evaluation, and Treatment of Attention-Deficit/Hyperactivity Disorder in Children and Adolescents." *Pediatrics* 144, no. 4 (October 2019): e20192528. doi.org/10.1542/peds.2019-2528.

Wyman, Peter A., Wendi Cross, C. Hendricks Brown, Qin Yu, Xin Tu, and Shirley Eberly. "Intervention to Strengthen Emotional Self-Regulation in Children with Emerging Mental Health Problems: Proximal Impact on School Behavior." *Journal of Abnormal Child Psychology* 38, no. 5 (July 2010): 707–720. doi.org/10.1007/s10802-010-9398-x.

Yeniad, Nihal, Maike Malda, Judi Mesman, Marinus H. van IJzendoorn, Rosanneke A. G. Emmen, and Mariëlle J. L. Prevoo. "Cognitive Flexibility Children across the Transition to School: A Longitudinal Study." *Cognitive Development* 31 (July–September 2014): 35–47. doi.org/10.1016/j.cogdev.2014.02.004.

INDEX

A

Attention Deficit Hyperactivity Disorder (ADHD)
- combined presentations of, 126
- diagnosis of, 4, 16, 88
- emotional control struggles and, 5
- as running in families, 106
- self-starters, children with ADHD as, 6

Attention Span
- color exercises, expanding through, 94, 133, 149
- counting games, sustaining attention in, 91, 97
- everyday strategies to build attention, 89
- focus, maintaining, 92, 93, 95, 96, 99, 100, 101
- goal-oriented persistence and sustained attention, 6, 11, 13
- in hierarchy of executive skills, 5, 17
- improving the attention span, 87
- kitchen activity for the inner chef, 116
- Make It Match, sustaining attention during, 54
- math games and concentration skills, 97, 98
- mindful awareness in guided meditation, 102
- music activity to enhance attention span, 90
- task initiation skills, building on, 109, 118

Attention to Detail, 8, 55, 94, 149

B

Brain
- biological factors, considering, 1, 9
- brain fatigue and concentration, 89, 92
- clear thinking after taking a break, 122
- details, helping the brain to remember, 61
- developing brain, not asking too much of, 103, 145, 159
- differences between adult and child brains, 20
- impulse control, training the brain for, 41
- medication effect on the brain, 88
- overwhelm, too many details contributing to, 60
- prefrontal cortex, role of, 5, 17, 107
- Same, Same, Different, slowing down brain activity with, 43
- self-motivation in the growing brain, 123
- visual and written notes, brain focus aided by, 97

D

Directions, following, 7, 34, 52, 53, 131

E

Emotional Control, 67
- catch, playing to build emotional control, 72
- consistent practice in the home, 85
- emotional awareness, enhancing, 70, 76
- emotional experiences, exploring, 82
- everyday strategies to build emotional control, 69
- feelings, connecting to behaviors, 71
- in Feelings Scavenger Hunt, 77
- in follow the leader game, 113
- grounding as a coping strategy, 74
- help, learning to ask for, 83–84
- in hierarchy of executive skills, 5–6
- mental flexibility, pairing with, 163, 165, 177
- mindfulness as a technique for, 42, 102, 153
- music, connecting to emotions, 73
- pausing and thinking before responding, 78
- in Rescue Mission exercise, 137
- task initiation as a tool for, 114
- uncomfortable emotions, coping with, 75
- validation as helping to maintain, 162
- working memory, using for, 54

Emotional Regulation, 9, 10, 12–13, 17
frustration tolerance and, 8
patience, exercise in strengthening, 34
self-soothing as helpful for, 74
turn-taking as aiding with, 7
working memory overload and, 50
Executive Skills, 14, 17, 21, 29, 179
assessment sheets, 10–11, 12–13
benefits of working on, 16
defining, 4–7
development in children, 8–9
role-modeling of, 15
supplemental skills, 7–8
See also Flexibility; Impulse Control; Memory Work; Organization

F

Feelings Forecast exercise, 80–81
Flexibility, 7, 11, 13, 27, 89, 162, 175
in Bending the Rules exercise, 164
cognitive flexibility, 161, 177
color games, flexible thinking in, 115, 166
emotional control skills, pairing with, 77, 165, 174, 177
in Flexible or Firm? activity, 169
in hierarchy of executive skills, 7, 8, 17, 177
impulse control and, 36, 114, 116, 170
mental flexibility, 8, 163, 168, 172, 173, 174, 177
organization games for, 167
planning and prioritization, aiding with, 171
task initiation and, 115, 117, 119
Trust Me activity, gaining practice with, 176
Focus For Fun exercise, 100
Frustration Tolerance, 8, 21, 59, 149

G

Goal-Oriented Persistence
in Don't Let It Drop game, 99
emotional control, learning, 54, 102
in A Fidget For Focus, 101
in hierarchy of executive skills, 5, 17
impulse control practice for, 91, 93, 102, 116
sustained attention and, 6, 11, 13, 90, 91, 92, 93, 94, 95, 96, 98
task initiation skills, strengthening, 90, 102, 109, 116, 118
working memory skills and, 54, 90, 94, 96, 97, 133

I

Impulse Control, 10, 12, 32, 46
in Acting On Emotion activity, 71
attention, sustaining, 8, 90, 91, 99, 101, 102
in Bending the Rules game, 164
color exercises, displaying in, 41, 152, 166
emotional control and, 72, 73, 74
everyday strategies to build, 33
food-related activities, practice with, 37, 38, 39, 93, 146
freeze games as helping with, 36, 112
in hierarchy of executive skills, 5, 17
mindfulness as aiding with, 31, 44, 90
in planning and prioritization skills, 129, 131, 134
reading skills, incorporating with, 40
self-control, strengthening, 34, 45
slowing down to control impulses, 35, 42
in stop-and-think exercise, 43
task initiation and, 111, 113, 114, 116, 147
turn-taking, gaining ability in, 7
working memory and, 56, 60, 78, 128, 150, 170
Individualized Education Program (IEP), 26

L

Let's Plan a Party! activity, 61

M

Memory Work
in Bending the Rules activity, 164
cleanup activities, engaging memory in, 131, 148
color exercises, memory work during, 52, 94, 133, 166
follow games, using memory in, 53, 170
guessing games, memory use during, 60, 63
impulse control and, 56, 112

math memory games, 62, 97, 98, 173
memory retention exercise, 55
mixing and matching activities, 54, 150
opposites and similarities, exercises in, 43, 168
planning exercises and, 128, 132, 136, 140
preparation activities, 64, 128, 136
reading activities, memory work in, 40, 50, 130
in scavenger and treasure hunts, 58, 77
self-control activities, 38, 45
in Spell It Out activity, 59
task initiation and, 117, 156
uncomfortable emotions, dealing with, 75, 78, 82, 166
working memory, 5, 8, 11, 13, 17, 49, 50, 51, 65

Motivation
Colors of Three, self-motivation in, 115
in Hide-and-Seek with Stuffies game, 110
intrinsic motivation, 24–25, 106, 107, 123
motivation assessment, 23
task initiation and, 6, 10, 12, 107
understanding motivation, 22
in Whatever You Say game, 113

O

Organization, 9, 10, 12, 144, 145, 159
checklist use in getting organized, 154
colors, organizing by, 146, 152
find-it game, learning organization through, 147
in hierarchy of executive skills, 5, 6–7, 17, 143
impulse control and, 39
independence, gaining with organizational abilities, 148
laundry skills, learning, 150
Let's Journal! activity, extending organization to, 158
mental flexibility as part of, 167
mindfulness and organizing your thoughts, 153
The Organization Challenge exercise, 156–157
Organize for a Cause activity, 151
predictability, organization helping to create, 149
Visual Reminders to get things done, 155

P

Parental Frustration, 21
Planning and Prioritizing, 6, 11, 13, 125, 127
fort building, planning skills used in, 134
in hierarchy of executive skills, 5, 8, 17
needs and wants, distinguishing between, 135
positive reinforcement for following a plan, 131
preparation activities, practicing, 64, 128
in The Quicksand Game, 129
in Rescue Mission activity, 137
self-control as part of, 38
short- and long-term goals, exploring, 140
skill improvement, ripple effects of, 141
storytelling, as part of, 130
teacher's class schedule, planning, 132
weather, responding to changes in, 136, 171
in What's the Game Plan? activity, 133

Positive Techniques, 19, 163, 175
in Change for Positive Choices game, 174
in Follow the Flexible Leader activity, 170
intrinsic motivation, instilling positive thoughts with, 24
planning and organizing, positive ripple effects of, 141
positive approach, importance of taking, 20–22
positive mindset, maintaining, 21, 24, 25, 159, 167
positive reinforcement as key, 27, 131, 179
validation and positive changes in children, 162

Problem-Solving, 7, 8, 16
in The Quicksand Game, 129
in Stacks of Snacks exercise, 39
working memory and, 11, 13, 58, 60, 62, 63

R

Reactive Attachment Disorder (RAD), 32

T

Task Initiation, 6, 9, 10, 12, 107, 123
- building blocks, use of, 111
- charades, task initiation as part of, 114
- in coloring activities, 115, 166
- in A Fidget for Focus activity, 101
- flexible thinking, importance of, 164
- following a plan, practice in, 131
- in guessing game, 108
- in hierarchy of executive skills, 5, 17
- how to start tasks, learning, 105
- kitchen activity, displaying in, 116
- new ideas, exploring, 117, 118
- obstacle course, putting together, 119–120
- in Opposite Day exercise, 168
- organization activities, 147, 148, 151, 153, 154, 156
- originality, incorporating into, 110, 112
- in Parent Interview activity, 121
- self-initiation, role in, 109, 113
- Visual Reminders, creating, 155

Teachers, how to work with, 26

Trauma-Focused Cognitive Behavioral Therapy (TF-CBT), 32

Turn-Taking, 7, 53

Acknowledgments

I would like to take a moment to acknowledge my incredible Mamaw Bo, who sadly passed away while I was working on this project. So many of my fondest childhood memories were spent "across the mountain." From making biscuits from scratch to wading barefoot in the creek, the times I spent with her were always my favorite. Mamaw was always one of my biggest fans, and now I know she's cheering me on from the best seat in the house.

About the Author

Melissa Rose, LPC-MHSP, NCC, is a board-certified, licensed professional counselor who specializes in children and families. Melissa is passionate about childhood mental health and owns a therapy practice exclusively dedicated to kids. She enjoys empowering families with knowledge and support so that they may find fulfillment and joy in parenting again. Melissa lives in East Tennessee with her husband and two sweet daughters, who all share a love for the outdoors and the Tennessee Volunteers.

Printed in the USA
CPSIA information can be obtained
at www.ICGtesting.com
CBHW040128120424
6439CB00011B/3

9 781638 787471